Off to a Bad Start

Off to a Bad Start

Chicken Soup for the Sold

by

John Blesso

Silk City Press
Hoboken, NJ

Silk City Press
225 Washington Street, Suite 1
Hoboken, NJ 07030

Layout and cover design: Jennifer Karp
Cover photo: Gail Thacker

ISBN 0-9654452-0-8 12.95

Library of Congress Catalog Card Number: 96-92544

Printed in the United States of America

First Edition
(Will be worth hundreds of dollars)

Acknowledgements

The author would like to thank:

Hélène Andrawiss
Stanislav Anikan
Alex Balk
Joyce Bergami
Catherine Best
Francis Blesso
Francis Blesso, Jr.
Jacqueline Blesso
Matthew Blesso
Margaret Carlson
Elizabeth Crowell
Keith Dixon
M. Dorian
Josh Frank
Jennifer Karp
Nancy Kern
Michael Mark
Ed McCoyd
Anne Oculy
Jodi Reamer
Tom Rudegeair
Kim Russello
Dave Russo
Lara Semones
David Suisman
Greg Sullivan
Gail Thacker
Juliet Traum
Jennifer Webster
Leighan White
Scott White
The Authors Guild

CONTENTS

NOTICE: THESE ARE NOT SHORT STORIES.
The episodes in this book are intended to be read in the order in which they appear.

"All these people [Americans] whose destiny is mass-produced are haunted by dreams of escape."
—*Simone de Beauvoir*

Side One

A Half-Dozen Hail Marys

I was nine years old the day Ronald Reagan was inaugurated. We froze our asses off playing two-hand touch during recess and then they made all 40 of us crowd around this tiny TV. I couldn't see anything, but shit, it was better than learning. That afternoon, I went to Dominic's house across the street to play Monopoly. But halfway through the game we got bored and went on a tear hunting through the old stuff in his attic. We stumbled over this wicked army footlocker. Dominic said it must have belonged to his dad and we practically broke our fingers trying to flip the latches open.

"What the fuck is that?" I said.

"Ho-ly *Shit!*" Dominic exclaimed, lifting out a pile of magazines with women on the covers. The footlocker was filled to the brim with copies of *Hustler* and *Club* and *Penthouse* going back to 1974.

"I guess they're my dad's," Dominic said, like he couldn't believe it. Dominic's dad was the mayor of our town, Lodensack, NJ.

Now, except for the girls we used to play doctor with, I had never seen a woman's pussy before. Then all of a sudden I'm staring at this monstrous woman with long dark curly hair and the only thing she's wearing is a white fur coat and a string of pearls and she's lying on her back and her knees are bent and her legs are spread apart and she's reaching around both of her thighs, spreading the sides apart. Her pussy didn't look anything like the little-girl pussies that looked like when you press your thumb against your hand—I mean I knew they had hair down there, but all of the folds and layers were so intricate, like a crumpled piece of red velvet, and as mysterious as a dark cave. I guess it scared me a little because I thought that women only wanted to have sex when they wanted to get pregnant. But here was this woman completely offering herself, and shit, I didn't even know magazines like that existed. My hands shook as I turned the pages in disbelief. But by the time I had turned to the next woman, my fear had turned to fascination.

After flipping to the end I looked up at Dominic. He had raced through 5 or 6 mags. I don't know what he was in such a hurry for. I mean, they were his father's—he could look at them whenever he wanted. As I watched him turning the pages in a frenzy, I thought it was kind of messed up that Dominic's father kept a stack of porno mags. I mean, he knows the governor and they got a picture over their fireplace of him *with the Pope* and, you know, you wouldn't think such a respected public figure would have this kind of stuff hidden away in his attic. But Dominic didn't seem to care. He looked up and we stared at the incredible pile of mags in the chest and I think we both realized we wouldn't be wasting our time playing Monopoly any more. I stuck a *Cheri* and a *Hustler* in the waistband of my shorts and we crept back down to his room. I smuggled them back to my house underneath the game board in the Monopoly box.

My mom was still watching the inauguration, so I went straight up to my room. My fingers began to twitch again as I stared at the magazines, carefully turning the pages like if they were antique bibles, believing that like pizza, this was something I would never outgrow. I would keep these two treasures until I was eighteen and could buy my own. But after a few weeks I did get bored of the same pictures. So I went back to Dominic's house to "play Monopoly" again. I returned the mags I used up and checked out two new ones. Back at home, I turned all the pages of one and then the other and then back to the first one, going a little slower and absorbing them over and over like when I got two new 45's from Kmart.

I took my Wonder Bread ruler out of my desk and measured my dick. Three inches long, if I held the ruler underneath. It would stay hard until my mother called me down to dinner and then I'd stare at the crucifix over my bed and think about Jesus hanging off the cross and how much it must have hurt and this usually got it down. Then after dinner it was right back upstairs until *The Incredible Hulk* came on channel 2 at eight o'clock. Sometimes I even skipped Hulk and once or twice I even skipped the *Dukes of Hazzard*, which came on right after—I'm surprised my mom didn't get suspicious because they were my favorite shows.

St. Jude's let us out half-day on the first Friday of every month. I'd run home and pack up the Monopoly box and head over to Dominic's to borrow new mags, and usually he didn't make me do too much stuff for them. But I started to get worried when it came time for me to make my First Confession. It was a Tuesday night and they made the church real dark inside. And when it was my turn, I spread the red velvet curtain and kneeled down on the wooden pew. Through the screen I could only see a waxy shadow and I wasn't sure who it was. I couldn't remember if *I* was supposed to start or what. Soon the shadow spoke and I recognized Father Izzy's voice and he told me to say an *Act of Contrition*. Sister Tina made us memorize the *Act of Contrition.* I had it down with my mother the night before, but I choked and screwed it up on the third line. I started over, but then I messed it up a second time.

"Why don't I give you an easier one," Father Izzy said.

"Okay," I said, a little confused.

"All you have to say is, "Have mercy on me, Lord, for I am a sinner."

"*That's it?*"

"That's all you need."

Father Izzy was so cool. If I ever became a priest, I'd be like him.

Have mercy on me, Lord, for I am a sinner.

I memorized his *Act of Contrition* right on the spot, thinking that was just like Sister Tina—making you learn a whole freaking paragraph when all you needed was one line. So I said it and then I didn't know what to say. I mean I knew—it wasn't like I was weak in the sin department—I just didn't know what I could say to Father Izzy. He was new at St. Jude's and definitely on the young side for a priest. Me and my mom liked him the best, but this also made it harder to tell him stuff. The magazines were the obvious sin, but there was no way I could confess that during the first go-around. I didn't want to get off to a bad start and I figured that for the first time, you should just get warmed up with some bullshit. So I told him about fighting with my brother and he gave me a little spiel about loving him and all and he called my brother by his name which kind of freaked me out. And then he asked me what else, and I didn't know what else to say. So I told him I ripped off ten dollars from my mother's purse to play craps with Dominic and some of the older kids, even though it wasn't true. He didn't seem to think it was that big of a deal, especially when I told him I hadn't rolled the dice yet, so he told me to just put the money back and say twelve *Hail Marys* and never do it again and try not to fight with my brother.

Since I never took the money, I didn't have to put it back. And since it was a sin I never committed, I figured I only owed six *Hail Marys*. I said them in my head during the commercials of *Diff'rent Strokes*, finishing them halfway through the second commercial break. I got up to take a leak and when I got back my brother was lying on the good couch. Usually I'd grab one of his ankles and yank him off, which was fun to do anyway, but for my Penance I just let him lie there.

I went to Confession once a month, because they let you out of religion class if you wanted to go and I hated religion class the most. But they didn't hike us over to the church to do it—we did it right in Father Izzy's office, sitting on chairs with the lights on. I mean, did they really expect me to unload all of this perverted shit right to his face? My deepest revelation to Father Izzy was that I threw snowballs at cars. I mean I know they're like sworn to secrecy and all, but he shakes hands with my mom and me on the steps after church. And my mom would definitely see something in his eye—she's a real pro at that stuff—and she'd assume the worst. And isn't all that secrecy stuff just for when the police asked questions? I could never keep it straight. Anyway, I never warmed up to confessing the magazines. And the more times I didn't mention it, the harder it got, because then he'd ask me how long I'd been doing it and I'd have to tell him and then that would be like a whole new sin in itself. But even if I had the balls to tell Father Izzy about the magazines, it wouldn't have done a lick of good—because I knew all of the *Hail Marys* in the world weren't going to *stop* me from looking at them. So I just kept on doing it. And after a while I stopped thinking about it.

Last year, when I was 13, I got Confirmed during the buzz of the '84 elections. My mom didn't like Reagan, but I thought he was OK because he liked Bruce and Dirty Harry. Dominic's dad was up for re-election also. I had no idea what was going on except everyone knew Nicky's dad would win again sure as Reagan was going to kick Mondale's ass. Anyway, by this time last year, Dominic had catalogued the whole footlocker on 3 x 5 cards. I mean, he was just short of his own Dewey Decimal System. I had been through a solid chunk of the footlocker myself, but my Confirmation pledge remained tacked up in the back of my mind as I watched Dominic locate a *Hustler* from 1978 and turn to a spread he wanted to show me. When the bishop said, "I denounce Satan and all his works," I was kind of nervous about saying "I do" because obviously I don't. But everyone else said it and I didn't think I was any better or worse than anybody else, so I said "I do" along with the rest of them.

"Look!" Dominic pointed at the *Hustler* he had found.

"You can actually *see* it going in."

"Holy shit," I said, grabbing the magazine from his hands.

"Do you want to check it out?"

"I do," I said.

At home, I tried to imagine when I would ever get around to doing some of the things I saw in the mags. I figured seventeen, if I was lucky. And that seemed cool because it was only four years away. Reagan's face came up on the news and I remembered four years earlier when I was nine and Reagan was inaugurated and me and Dominic first found the mags.

That didn't seem too long ago, so I figured I'd probably be getting down and dirty while the Gipper was still in the saddle. But after a few days, seventeen seemed like forty years away. I *wanted* sex. My dick had doubled in size hard and soft and pubes curled around either side of it, almost joining over the top like a dark halo. Hair covered my nuts like barbed wire and for some reason, I found myself twisting and grabbing it as I turned the pages.

Near the back of the *Hustler* there was an ad for one of those plastic dicks. It never made any sense to me that there was even a market for these things. Did there really exist women who couldn't find someone to have sex with them? Christ, I'd fuck anything that squats to pee. So this ad was only about the size of a postage stamp, and the woman held the thing between her legs and she had her ass up in the air and both of her holes were wide open and she looked like she was begging and moaning for it. And I squinted at the ad thinking, if only I could find this woman, I'd fucking give it to her all day long; I'd put Krazy Glue on my dick so you could never take it out and it killed me that she's out there somewhere and I'm here and God there's gotta be tons of women like that and where the fuck are they and *Jesus!* I just wanted *cunt!* My hips started humping the bed, and I imagined I was fucking her and I started going on like automatic pilot, really giving it to the bedsheet, staring at her longing expression and her arched back and her gaping holes and how bad she wanted it and it started to burn against the bedsheet but I couldn't stop myself and I wondered if I was going to come but that couldn't happen until you had your first wet dream but I'm so fucked up anyway and then I *knew* I was going to come and I got scared and ran to the bathroom, squeezing my dick so I wouldn't squirt it all over the walls and thank God my mother wasn't upstairs and my heart thumped as three cloudy drops inched out and fell into the toilet.

Three days later I turned to the same picture and tried doing it again, but my dick got all burned up against the bedsheet and I gave up.

The next day, I began eighth grade at St. Jude's and I checked out two new mags from Dominic. I didn't tell him I'd shot a load. He was two years older than me and if anything like that happened to him, he never said anything about it. In fact, he didn't really talk about sex at all anymore. But he'd practically worn out the whole footlocker. I couldn't believe it. I mean there must've been three hundred mags there. Anyways, I found this one spread in *Club* of this blond woman with really big tits and a shaved pussy and I raced home. My mom had mixed me up a glass of Quik, an act she had committed herself to every afternoon since I came home from the first day of Kindergarten at St. Jude's. I grabbed it and headed for the stairs.

"Giuseppe! Where are you going with *that*?"

I didn't even see her. When I turned around, I couldn't tell if she was pointing at the Quik or the Monopoly box.

"Upstairs," I said, getting my shit together and trying to sound like I was annoyed that she called me Giuseppe, which she always did when she was pissed.

"It's hot as blazes upstairs," she said.

I looked at her as though heat wasn't something that mattered.

"You know, I'm in eighth grade now. You don't have to mix me up Quik any more." I couldn't believe I had been struck by a boldness attack while I was standing there holding a Monopoly box jam-packed with items that would make my mom shit. "If I want some, I can mix it up myself," I said kind of half-assed. "I'm big enough now."

"I guess you are," she sighed. "Just be careful."

"I promise." I said.

It was 97 degrees outside and hot as Hell in my room. I put the Quik on my nightstand and I didn't even bother putting the Monopoly board back in the box. I flipped through all the pages first, realizing that my technique for studying the mags was in fact that thing with the three R's every teacher tries to teach you—it never worked—but I always had trouble reading. Midway through the *Club* I came across the spread with the shaved blond that had caught my eye. She dug her fingers in her pussy and you could see the whole thing all spread apart like she was going to dissect it or something. And in the second to last picture, she was on her hands and knees in front of a mirror with her middle finger all the way inside and when I looked down, my dick was purple and I was squeezing it really hard, but I guess it felt good and Christ I was burning up in the heat and you could see the woman's face in the mirror and in the next picture she clenched her teeth like she'd just tore into a drumstick and she held herself up with one hand and pressed one of her tits up against her and the other one hung down and it looked really huge and I was sweating like crazy and her cunt was spread apart all pink and it looked like a butterfly about to fly away or a comfortable couch you could just sink right into and my dick was all sweaty and hard as a rock and bent over funny like a handle on a suitcase and it was like I was giving myself an Indian rope burn and God her cunt looked so good and I wanted to just disappear inside it and *GOD!*

My head spun and the room looked fuzzy and my body felt like it was being beamed up to a spaceship. It was like I was asleep and awake at the same time and I don't know how long I was lying there, but when I sat up, big blobs of it lay on my sheets, which my mom had just changed. I wiped it up but three wet circles remained. I didn't know if it stained or not and when I bent over to smell it I figured it did. God, it smelt horrible—like a cleaning product or something—it didn't smell like anything that should come out of the human body.

I mopped my brow and grabbed the glass of Quik. As I took a chocolatey sip, I knew what I had to do. I filled my mouth with Quik and then dribbled it out over the circles. I rubbed it in like I had tried to clean it and then I hid the mags and went downstairs.

"Mom?" I said in an ascending tone to buff her up that she wasn't going to be happy.

"*Yes?*"

"You're gonna kill me."

"*What?!*"

"I spilled."

"Giuseppe! Didn't I *tell* you?" She sighed. "Did you clean it up?"

"Yeah, but some got on my sheets."

"I *just* changed them."

"I'm sorry. I'll put them in the hamper and put new ones on."

"Yes, you *will*."

That night, I took my dirty school shirt, the sky-blue collared kind they make you wear with the same dorky tie since Day One at St. Jude's, and laid it out on my bed. I turned to the same woman and hocked a loogie into my palm and it worked much better. When I was done, I mopped off the shirt and then deposited it in the hamper, rubbing the spot up against the Quik stain on the soiled sheet before closing the lid.

I began doing it quite often, learning to aim it onto a folded tissue. When I got up to two or three times a day, I started to get worried because I read that it was wrong in one of those orange pamphlets with the bubble head stick figures. I tried stopping. But then I couldn't stop thinking about it, which made me worry about it even more than when I was actually doing it. Finally, I'd break down after a couple of days and God, I'd come like crazy.

Of course I never confessed my "self-pollution" or whatever they called it to Father Izzy. Shit, I never even said anything about the magazines. I mean how can you possibly talk about this with a guy who's never even done it? What the fuck are you supposed to do? Sex before marriage is wrong. Whacking off is wrong. They never said anything about blowjobs, and I thought about trying to get a girl to give me one once in a while. But I wouldn't know where to get one for starters. And you can't really force a girl to give you a blowjob, because she'd probably bite it off.

If They Shot Four More...

If they shot four more, we'd have the whole week off!" I laughed at the punchline even though I had heard George's joke before.

"We should start with that one right there." John the biker pointed at Clarence, the black lab technician passing in front of the breakroom in his white coat.

"I tink it puts a bug up your ass, John, havin a college-educated nigger higher up then you," Sal said.

"I could give a fuck how high up he is. The Water Company has already got three niggers too many."

"Come on, John, Clarence is a good guy." George blew out a stream of smoke.

"He's a *fucking nigger*," John spat from under his dirty blond moustache.

"But he's a regular guy. He doesn't cause any trouble around here." George stubbed out his Marlboro in a Snapple cap. "And it's not like he's going to be moving in on *your* job."

We nodded and laughed.

John pulled a hunting knife from his hip and slit the seam of the label on his Snapple bottle. “I guess I didn’t realize you guys were such nigger lovers,” he said, flicking the brown label from its bare shell onto the red gingham table cloth.

“Clarence’s alright,” George continued. “He’s not one of those black nation fuckers running around screaming about their blackness and all. I mean, he keeps to himself and he’s polite and doesn’t act up and doesn’t fuck with anything.”

The other guys stared at John. He didn’t say anything.

“They’re not *all* bad.” George said.

“Like I said,” John intoned, “I didn’t realize you were such a nigger lover.”

“I aint no goddamned nigger lover so stop saying that I am!” George stood, his face flushed as he craned his head around to see if anyone was in the hallway. “Look, I got a black guy moved in next door to me,” he spoke under his breath. “He believes in Jesus and he pays taxes like the rest of us. He’s O.K. We even watched a Giants game together once.” His expression cracked with a flash of regret at his last admission. It was news to me, too. Believe me, I heard all about it when the black family moved in next door to him, but he never said nothing about watching football with the guy.

“Look, he’s *OK*. Once we were both finishing up our lawns and he brought out a couple of beers and we sat down on my porch.”

Everyone was silent. John raised his eyebrows and folded his knife into its sheath.

“That’ll be the day,” John said, cramming his garbage through the neck of his empty Snapple bottle and screwing the cap back on. “That when a nigger moves next door to me—providing I didn’t shoot him first—that I’d *drink* with him. On my *front-fucking porch?!*” John’s face turned rose-red and then faded back to white. “I guess that’s the difference between you and me. There isn't good or bad. I'd fucking shoot them all. Dead."

"I'd shoot em all except Colin Powell," Sal added.

"I'd shoot that nigger dead in his fucking tracks," John said.

"Actually," Sal said, "I'd keep Colin Powell, Jordan, O.J. and everyone on that 'Martin' show."

John stared at Sal, disgusted.

"It's a funny show!" Sal said indignantly.

"Look, John," George cut back in. "I don't care what you say. There's a *difference*. You got your normal blacks and then you got your niggers. I hate niggers just as much as you, so don't be trying to make it like I don't. But there's a *fucking difference*!" he spat in a loud whisper.

"Whoa, take it easy," John said. "I didn't realize it meant so much to you."

A thick blue vein coursed through George's head. "The diffrence is people like Clarence are O.K. I love black people like him. They're well trained and they've got jobs and they don't go running around screaming about their blackness and the White Man and all of that bullshit. Like I said, if everyone was like Clarence, we wouldn't have this fucking problem. But that's never gonna happen. Sure's I got hair on my nuts there's always gonna be niggers. Don't you *fucking understand* it makes more sense to be nice to them and encourage more of them to be like Clarence and just *shut the fuck up*?"

The other men stared hard at George as though he had just unwrapped the clue to a puzzle they never expected to solve. Georgie went to J.C. for two years, but he packed it in six credits short of graduating. I don't know why he didn't just finish the two classes he needed for his junior degree—he was studying bookeeping and he probably could've gotten a good job, but he kept saying how at the Water Company you got job security, whereas bookeepers get laid off all the time. I don't know. I barely made it through one semester, but I sure as hell wouldn't have quit with just six credits to go. But I never wanted to go to college anyway. My older brother got recruited for a full ride at Rutgers to play baseball, but he was killed Labor Day weekend before the beginning of his first semester. It really busted up my father. So when I graduated high school the next year, I just kind of filled out the application with George and began classes in the fall. But my father never really got over my brother's death and I never really got down to studying, so I dropped out. I wasn't really cut out for that sort of thing—but Georgie was always real bright. Sometimes guys'll bust his chops about how going to college sucked all of the common sense out of his head, but when Georgie pipes up, they always cock an ear.

"Fuck all that and *fuck* you idiots," John scowled, scanning our faces.

"And I'd also keep that guy Henry's got working in his garage," Sal rambled on, oblivious. "Shit, he's got my Cougar running smooth as silk. I *tell* Henry to put him on the job cause you get a good mechanic, you don't fuck around..." Sal trailed off, noticing that everyone was staring at him.

"I'm wid you, John." One of the younger men stood behind John and gripped his shoulders. He hadn't worked that long at the Water Company—maybe eight years. He was the nephew of one of the Commissioners and he still squeezed into his high school football jacket. "We should shoot all the niggers," he said, shaking his head before walking out.

Sal sat back in his chair, counting off on his fingers: "Colin Powell, Jordan, The Juice, Clarence Thomas, the Martin show and Henry's mechanic. But that's *it*." Sal's walkie-talkie crackled and popped and Little Jimmy's voice came over: "Sal, monitor three is down."

"Asshole just drove in," Sal said to us.

Little Jimmy's this old guy who works the front gate and he warns us whenever the grounds supervisor decides to drop in. Busting our balls is about the only thing Asshole's got to keep himself busy. I mean, the guy's got a VCR in his office, for Chrissakes.

"On my way, Jimmy," Sal replied. He's a good guy, Little Jimmy. We worked in maintenance together when I first started at the Water Company, but he's a diabetic now and he's got these scabs all over because he can't get off the sugar. He arrives at the gatehouse every day with a half-dozen donuts and a large coffee with four sugars for breakfast. He says his doctor says he's killing himself, but then he says, Doctors, what do they know?

"I gotta get to purification," Sal said. He slapped his hands down on the table and rose with a groan. "So long, gentlemen."

Everybody else followed him out of the breakroom except John the biker, Marty, and myself. I didn't know if I should get up or not. John pushed himself up to a standing position and adjusted the tools hanging from a worn leather belt that bore his father's initials branded into the strap. He stared right at George until George looked away. John snatched up his Snapple bottle filled with garbage and dropped it into the recycling bin before stepping out. The clank of his tools and the slow thud of his steps resonated in the hallway as Georgie dug in his shirt for a Marlboro. George looked at me, shook his head and sped down the hall towards the locker room. Through the glass, I saw Asshole's car turn down the hill. I had to get out of there, but I didn't feel like going back to the pump station, so I headed out towards the gatehouse to drop in on Little Jimmy.

Some People Never Learn

I duct tape the used condom up on the wall and write down the date and the name and then I give a rating with stars, like they do with movies. I've screwed over half the second floor. Some of the women really hate me. But why should I care when I've got my own harem conveniently located on the floor below? It's a simple exchange—feelings or emotions are of little concern. Sure, a few of them get choked up after dropping crazy notions of trying to reform me, but I can't feel bad for them—they knew damn well what they were getting into.

At Gample University, my conquests are legendary—I'm as famous as the basketball players. Whenever I want sex, I go downstairs and knock on the door of my choice. Thirty seconds later, we're back in my room. They used to drop back, to avoid being seen with me. But then I would drop back, too. Once they realized this, I had them hurrying up to my room as though someone were chasing them.

If there are other people in the room, it takes longer. But if it's just guys, the other ones usually cheer the guy's name as he sets off on what they refer to as the "walk of shame." Once in a while a guy will say no—he's trying to move in on a girl in the dorm and he knows one of his friends will dutifully inform said girl of his departure with me. He'll shake his head and a church-like quiet falls across the room as the rest of them sit up straighter than the teacher's pet with the correct answer. I watch them squirm as I scan their faces, even though I already have my second choice worked out.

The best is when there's another girl in the room. Especially if my choice is trying to hook up. Hooking up can be such a formality. From borrowing notes, to calling, to finally going out and getting blasted—there's a lot of steps and maybe the odds aren't looking so hot. Once I went down for this one guy I hadn't fucked yet and just before I got to his door, I heard a girl's voice and then his—he was speaking in an odd tone. I knocked on his door—everyone knows my knock—three sharp loud raps—and he stopped talking mid-sentence, because he knew it was me and he was a me-virgin and his first reaction was to not answer the door.

"Aren't you going to get that?" the girl said.

Finally, he pulled open the door and I said his name. And he knew he could drop his frustrating quest and be fucking me up in my room quicker than it would take to cook a bag of microwave popcorn. "Yes?" he replied, with a look on his face like a little boy in need of a bathroom.

"Oh," I said, leaning into the room. "I didn't realize you were busy. Maybe I'll come back some other time." I didn't know the girl and I glanced at his face to see if my reputation preceded me. His face scrunched up as though I must be out of my mind to knock on *his* door, my goodness! So I suspected that he suspected that she had heard about me and as I closed the door I heard her whisper:

"Is that that girl who..." her voice trailed as I walked down the hall and landed three raps on my second choice's door.

Sure, I get off on watching them squirm. Why shouldn't I? You should hear the things they say about me. The exploits get wilder by the month. I mean, I pretty much do the same thing with every guy, but they start outdoing one another with stories of candlewax and dildos and all of this stuff that I'm not into. Then there's the stories about how I really prefer women, even though I've never been with a woman. And then there's the guys I've never chosen. Some of them badmouth me in lame attempts to appear pious in front of the girls they're trying to hook up with. "My God what a slut! I can't believe anyone would ever go with her, blah blah blah." Sometimes when I overhear these frustrated denunciations of my character, I'll make a mental note for a future knock—an early knock on a weeknight with lots of witnesses about so that Mr. Pious can't use the tired scapegoat of drunkenness as to how he ended up as exhibit A on my wall.

The cum turns translucent after a day and the condom shrivels. I burn incense and in the smoke I can faintly smell myself as I admire my wall. So far, there are eight rows in my collection this year. I've hung every condom—except one from this guy who stepped into his jeans with a stupid smile on his face and the used condom still on. He whooped it up as he ran down the hall, bragging to his friends about how I wouldn't get to tape him up. In its place I duct-taped a pencil that had been sharpened all the way down and wrote his name, the date and BOMB for his rating. He *was* a regular—I never knocked on his door again. And no one has given me shit about relinquishing the condom since.

About a month ago, I was sitting on my bed with my door open and I could hear two girls congregating in the hallway. It was pretty elaborate how they broke into idle chat coming from different directions. There's usually some sort of envoy at least once a month who thinks of an excuse to knock on my door. Notes or a calculator—excuses borrowed from the guys trying to hook up with them. They wanted to borrow my psych notes. I turned to dig them up, stealing a glance at their eyes scanning the wall. Sometimes it makes me feel like a bear in the zoo. But I took my sweet time and let them get an eyeful. It's incredible how a college education is but a pleasant, expensive formality for so many. *A four year spin on a hedonistic merry-go-round. All is a blur, yet a cloaked puritanism reigns throughout the chaos of the party, curtailing the libidos of those that, ironically, seem so bent on destroying themselves.* I wrote that yesterday. Obviously, I've thought about this a bit—I jot down stuff all the time, as I plan to write my thesis on this subject.

I spun back around, facing the girls and presented them with the notes they requested. "Please bring them right back," I said. "I get nervous if they're gone too long." I tossed my head from side to side.

"Sure. Thanks. We'll bring them right back."

I know you will, I thought to myself as they stepped out, breaking into hushed gossip in the hallway. Whether they were looking for their boyfriends on the wall or just something to talk about, I have no clue. But despite my non-traditional social life and all of the things they say about me, at least I'm here primarily to learn.

A few weeks ago, I returned late from the library the night before my psych mid-term. It was a Thursday night—the biggest party night at Gample. I put away my books and sat back on my bed and continued reviewing my psych notes until my mind wandered and I noticed the palm of my hand pressing down on the ridge of my pubis—sometimes my hand just ends up there. I unbuttoned my shirt and unhooked my bra, cupping my breasts, allowing my nipples to grow hard enough in the cool draft of the room so that I could just flick them with the tip of my tongue. I stuck my fingers beneath the rim of my underwear and teased out my clit. When it stood erect, I buttoned my shirt and buttoned my jeans and walked down to the second floor to reward myself after six hours in the library. Three guys hanging out in the hallway stood at attention as I neared them. Their backs flattened against the wall and then they slumped back to their loose conversation as though I wasn't there. I didn't know any of their names, but I gave them a quick inspection. The one who looked the least drunk also ranked the highest. A loose football jersey hung from his pecs and he had a cute face and an aquiline nose and delicate fingers that suggested a long, thin dick. He wore a Gample MENS BASKETBALL hat screwed all the way down with the bill curved around his eyes like a tunnel.

He'll do, I thought—I didn't exactly choose them for their personalities.

"Testaverdes?" I said.

He pointed at his chest and his eyebrows shot up. "Me?"

I rolled my eyes and turned and he trotted behind me. I could hear his fists punching the air.

"Do you know that in Latin your name roughly means 'Green Nuts'?"

"Huh? Oh, that's not me."

"Did you borrow that shirt?"

"No," he said. A bit defensive. I started to second-guess him, but once inside, the wall commanded his attention.

"It's clear," he said.

"You haven't figured that out yet?"

"I've never saved it," he smiled. I guess he'll be all right, I thought. He yanked out the hem of his jersey.

"Unh-uh," I said. "Shirt and socks stay on."

That was one of my rules. I didn't want any of their funky B.O. on my bed. He left his hat on, but I didn't say anything. I grabbed his round shoulders and slid my hands up to the muscles over his collarbone and he flexed them. He tried to kiss me, but I kept him at arm's length and slid my hands down to his chest and felt his well-rounded pecs. I looked down, confirming my earlier suspicion—he *was* big—after a while you can just tell. I undid his pants and tore open a Sheik Elite. His dick jumped when I touched it to roll the condom on. He sat back on my bed and I sat at the foot and massaged my breasts as I undressed. Then I played with my clit some more and his face scrunched up and I pulled him on top of me and guided it in. He slid in and out of me with a steady rhythm and I reached down again—I have to do this early on before they peter out. My hips bobbed and twitched as I brought myself off. It was good, but he kept going and I wondered if he wasn't too drunk to come. My hips stopped bobbing and I squinted over at my schedule and began to mentally plan my day around my psych midterm, thinking, Whenever you're ready. His eyes clenched shut and he kept going and then he began hitting it just right. My hips started moving and I thought he was going to make me come again all by himself. "Harder," I told him and he really started going and my head started to spin and "Fuck me harder!" I yelled.

I heard a distant ringing noise when I felt his hands around my neck.

"You *fucking* whore!" he grunted.

When I reached up to pull his hands away, he began to choke me.

"You *dirty, stinking, fucking WHORE!*" He pushed down on each word.

My eyes popped open in a rush of terror like I hadn't felt since the accident. He readjusted his hands and I took a quick suck of air and bit down on my lower lip and extended my legs, bringing my heels down into his back. He lost his wind and released my neck and I pushed him onto the floor.

"*You fucking maniac!*" I hoarsely mouthed like in a bad

dream when you have no voice. I groped my neck as I pulled on my bathrobe and yanked the door open, regaining my breath.

"YOU FUCKING MANIAC!" I screamed. A dozen people in the hallway rushed over, gaping inside at him, rolling on the floor, tangled up in his jeans with the Sheik Elite still wrapped around his waning erection.

I stepped back in and the high-pitched chirp of a whistle ripped through the hallway as Maryanne, the R.A. appeared.

"WHAT'S THE PROBLEM!" she screamed.

"He tried to strangle me!" I could see the red marks in the mirror on the far wall and I pulled my head to the side, exposing my neck to her.

"WHO DID?!" Maryanne demanded, wide-eyed and trembling.

"Who the fuck do you think?!" A girl in the crowd pointed at the guy as he brought himself to his feet.

"Bullshit," he crab-walked over to the door, still hunched over. "Sheesha fucking shlut...sheesha fucking liar..." He pulled down the bill of his Gample MENS BASKETBALL hat, further obscuring his eyes.

"OKAY! OKAY! OKAY!" Maryanne blew into her whistle again; long, then short. Her face was flushed and her lower lip trembled. "ALL RIGHT! EVERYBODY CALM DOWN! YOU!" she pointed at the guy, "COOL IT! AND YOU!" she pointed at me, hesitating as though trying to recall some standard procedure. "EVERYBODY CLEAR OUT!" she screamed, but no one moved and she blew into the whistle again until the cops came around the corner.

I aced my psych midterm and they listed his name in the POLICE NEWS column of the school newspaper. But you had to read between the lines to figure out that we were having to read between the lines to figure out that we were having sex. In the end they just put him on probation, relocated him to the Desert and gave him forty hours of community service.

I stuck with my regular knocks with a new rule: I was always on top. That way I remain in total control. I stuck to my rule, even though sometimes I really like the bottom. I can get myself off better from the top, but when someone else gives you an orgasm, it's just—I don't know—nicer? It was odd. But after the choking incident, my regular knocks seemed more considerate, often asking how I was doing. It was nice to chat once in a while, and I think they realized it was a pretty sweet deal for them and really I just wanted to be treated with respect. In the end, it was just sex. And anyone can have as much as they want if they weren't so worried about what their friends say.

I closed my notebook after a long study session and rolled some Sure under each arm before heading downstairs. No one was in the hallway so I didn't bother locking my door.

Independence Day

I dropped a tab of acid on the Fourth of July before setting out to mow the lawn. Independence Day 1995 fell on a Tuesday, but everyone celebrated it on Monday for the extended weekend. That pissed me off because you don't celebrate Christmas on the closest Monday—you celebrate it on December 25 no matter what day it falls on. You wouldn't ever compromise the birth of Jesus, and the birth of our nation is at least as important, but nobody at the Water Company or anywhere else had a problem sticking it on a Monday.

So what happened was last week? George's older brother found some tabs in his son's bookbag. He showed them to George and George showed them to me.

"Looks like acid," I said.

George called his brother back and he was on the phone for like a half-hour, lighting one Marlboro off the butt of another while trying to convince his older brother not to turn his own son over to the cops. But Georgie was pretty tight about that stuff, too. He never tripped or got stoned even.

Back in high school, he used to go on about how it causes brain damage and all, but I never believed any of that. I dropped the tabs in my shirt pocket and we both forgot about them.

My wife was commemorating Independence Day by shopping with her friends and she was gone for the evening. At the barbecue yesterday we all got a little *too* patriotic and everyone was all partied out and Georgie took his boys to the Stadium and so I figured I might as well mow the lawn since it needed mowing and my mind hadn't been bent out of whack in years and there wasn't much else to do anyway.

I placed a single tab on the tip of my tongue and began ripping up the weeds in my back yard. I hadn't done acid since senior year in the fall of '79. Back then we all heard stories from the older kids about how tripping can expand your mind and all, but we took it for what it was: a good time. After the weeds, I plugged in the trimmer and leveled the flattops of my bushes and shrubs. An hour later, I still couldn't feel anything, so I took the other hit, remembering all the bullshit pieces of paper that used to go around in high school.

I felt a mild body high as I bent over to pull the starter. The mower roared to life and the gas smelt good. Halfway through the back yard, the tips of the grass flopped over, taking on an attractive silvery glow and my hands on the vibrating mower started to feel a little further off. It felt good and I kept mowing even rows and by the time I was through with the back, the lawn lost its silvery color as the fresh clipped grass stood at attention in a sea of green. The garage shimmied out of focus and when I zoomed back in, the white aluminum siding rippled with that familiar warble, expanding as I drew a deep breath and then contracting as I exhaled. When I looked up, the edge of the roof stood out against the deep blue sky as though it had been cut out and pasted in place.

The neighbors had a barbecue going and it smelt real good and my stomach started juicing with that raw strychnine burn, as I pushed the mower past my neighbor's new Nissan in the driveway. Nissans are nice cars. They're sporty and good on gas. I even thought about buying one once, but they would never let me hear the end of it at the Water Company for buying a Japmobile and don't I support America blah blah blah meanwhile they're all ready to adjust the celebration of the most important holiday we got to whatever day fits their schedule, like it's some kind of faggy lunch date or something. Fuck them. I made a mental note to wax my car.

A cool breeze caught the branches of the oak tree across the street. God, it was beautiful. I never realized it before. I mean it was just a big, beautiful fucking tree. Nice thick sturdy branches. The branches gently rocked and like the whole thing swayed a little and the leaves were so fucking green and goddamnit, it was just a beautiful sight and I couldn't believe I never really appreciated it before. My neighbor across the street waved hello to me and I waved back and he folded his arms and just stared at me. I worried that I made a crooked row and I looked behind me but the lawn looked fine and when I looked back, he was putting a key in the door of his Chevy Lumina.

I finished the lawn and stood and admired it for a second, but not as long as I would have liked to. Then I wheeled the mower back into the garage and went up to the bathroom and stripped naked. I turned on the shower, but just before stepping in, I saw that my mustache and sideburns could use a trim, so I buzzed them real close. I was about to get in again when my gut expanded in the mirror and I figured that since I was dirty and sweaty, I might as well go lift some weights. So I went down to the basement to do a few sets of curls. In the warbling mirror I thought I could see through my naked flabby frame at the trim body I had when I was a halfback in flabby frame at the trim body I had when I was a halfback in high school. The middles of my eyes were black and I didn't quite look like myself—more like someone who resembled me—a distant cousin or something.

The water was still running when I got back upstairs and it felt good. My skin felt like it had an extra coating and I had some trouble recalling my cleaning lineup. Shampoo, conditioner, soap? I wasn't sure if I had the right bottles, and I elbowed a row of health and beauty aids off the shelf. God, my wife had a half a CVS behind our shower door alone. I located a familiar looking bottle, but my fingers felt weak and numb flipping open the top and the shower head looked like a snake coming out of the wall and I scrubbed myself pink because it seemed like I couldn't get all the grime off.

Downstairs, the food in the refrigerator floated in fluorescent space and I grabbed a tall can of Miller High Life—I was too cheap to shell out for those imported bullshits in the green bottles that George buys, but Miller is made the American way and that's gotta count for something, doesn't it? I popped open the beer and stepped out in my backyard to admire my freshly cut lawn and the grass felt *wonderful* sprouting up between my toes so green and when I looked down, I realized I didn't have any clothes on and I bolted back inside, hoping nobody saw me. I was still dripping from the shower. I dashed back upstairs, dried off and zipped up some jeans without any underwear. I put on my navy-blue Yankee tee with the white 23 on the back and cautiously stuck my head out the door.

The mint leaves on the edge of the garden smelt fresh. I must have clipped some with the mower and they smelt so good that I chugged the rest of my beer and dumped a tray of ice in a pitcher for iced tea. I went out back and the lawn was a green pond, like you could just dive right in it and drown. I yanked out a clump of leaves, but the roots came out and I ran back inside. As hard as I pulled, I couldn't separate the roots from the bunch of leaves so I grabbed the scissors and cut them. I ran them under the sink and dumped the whole bunch in the pitcher along with a couple of scoops of iced tea and mixed it all up with a wooden spoon. It was like a brown sea of green spinning around and I stared at it for some time. My fingers still weren't working right, and not all the iced tea was mixing up. So I stuck my hand in and swished it around some more and then gave it a shot of lemon juice and it was good. God, I hoped the neighbors didn't call the cops on me.

I unwrapped a package of chicken breasts and dumped them on the grill and slopped some Bar-B-Q sauce on top and ran back inside. I stood by the door and I could still smell the mint leaves. So fresh. I ventured back out for another bunch to clean off and laid the leaves on top of the Bar-B-Q sauce on the chicken.

The rushes were really coming on, so I stumbled back inside and crashed down in my La-Z-boy and turned on the national news which was playing a commercial for Preparation-H. The guy who was promising to shrink my hemorrhoidal swelling started coming off the screen, like the TV was a stage, and for a minute, it seemed like he was talking right at me, like he was watching me. Finally, the news came back on and they did a story about a heatwave in Chicago that wiped out all of these people. My hands still felt funny and I started wrenching my fingers until they played a commercial for Ex-Lax and then a commercial for Met Life and then one for Geritol and then the news came back and they did a special feature on some of the children who were killed in the Oklahoma City bombing and Jesus Christ the whole fucking thing, commercials and all, was just about death and your ass. And I couldn't tell if I was just tripping too hard, or if the national news was fucked like that all the time.

The news finally ended and then Jeopardy! came on. I like watching Jeopardy! when my wife's not around, because she knows all the answers. She's a dental assistant, so she gets all the science and medicine questions. Plus her and her friend do the crossword every day at work, so she knows all that crap. That doesn't mean she's smarter than me just because I don't know the uh, capital of...Zimbabwe or whatever. Georgie's real smart and he don't know the answers on Jeopardy! neither. And the proof that deep down the people on Jeopardy! are idiots is that they don't know how to bet their money. Guy's down forty-five hundred bucks with three answers left and he bets twelve hundred on the daily double. I mean it's not rocket science, which I guess is the problem for most of those people. Still, I don't like sitting around like an idiot watching my wife zip half the answers when I don't even know where Katmandu is.

A big-time rush jarred my whole head and upper body and the TV screen started floating towards me and Alex Trebek's head started getting larger and the rest of the TV just kind of sank back in the darkness against the wall and so fucking what if I don't know who's the Chief Justice of the Supreme Court! I picked up the remote control and started zapping—enough Jeopardy!

I was about to zap CNN when the hot black woman with the funny lower lip who sounds three times as white as I do said something about the images are going to be graphic. I put the remote down and sat up in the chair. They showed these guys getting offed for real in some smoggy city and it was like they were zipping across the street and then pap pap pap pap and they were dead. The gunshots sounded like cap guns or popcorn popping and the screen looked grainy like a music video, but they were dead for real and it was like someone was watching me through the TV, trying to fuck with me, giving me death at every channel.

I smelled smoke and remembered my chicken and I looked at my watch and by the time I figured it out, I realized I had no idea what time it was when I put the chicken on. I ran out back and flipped it over. It was black, but I like it well done. I covered the charred side with more Bar-B-Q sauce and draped mint leaves on top. I stood in the kitchen and watched the clock spin for four minutes so I wouldn't miss the chicken and I never realized how loud the refrigerator is. In fact I never noticed the hum before at all. I didn't want to open it any more than I had to because all the food floating in fluorescent light freaked me out. I ran back outside and took the chicken off but the other side wasn't really done too well. I thought it would even out the burnt side so I put it in the microwave on high power for four minutes. When I took it out it was smoking and black around the corners.

My hands looked as raw and pink and stringy as the chicken and I worried that I shouldn't have taken that second tab. The rushes were coming on heavy and I puttered around the kitchen. The white appliances blended into the counter and began to look foreign as I tore into the chicken. I decided to sit down at the kitchen table and my wife's cat jumped up on the table. I hate the hairy little fucker—the only reason I got one was that we were having trouble conceiving. I bought it as a kitten for my wife's 30th birthday because it kind of depressed her to turn 30 without at least being pregnant, so I thought having something small and cuddly would help her be patient since I wasn't going to do any of that jerking off into test tubes business. But she'll be 32 in the fall and the cat's full grown. I picked it up and it started purring and I felt its warmth on my legs and watched its back rise and fall and I got back a sense of myself again. The cat planted a white paw on the edge of the table, eyeing the second chicken breast for the cat and she put a paw on top of it to hold it in place and attacked the meat with a fury like she was having some kind of kitty orgasm or something. Then I heard a scream and spun around with my hand on my heart, but it was only the neighbors. Betty was screaming at one of her kids and suddenly I was kind of glad I didn't have any. A lot of times the guys at the Water Company'll say stuff like: "Whatever you do, don't ever have any kids." And even though they say it like they're joking, I'm not so sure. If they could fold their arms and nod their heads like Barbara Eden in *I Dream of Jeannie* and just make their children disappear, would they do it? Because that's the impression I get—if they could do it all over, the big thing would be no children. But still, I really think it would be nice to have a couple of boys. Maybe a daughter, too.

For about a half-hour, I stared at the corner of a window George helped me put in the kitchen. You wouldn't think you could stare at the corner of a window for a half-hour, but for some reason, I was perfectly happy to do so. My wife was real happy with the window because of all the light but when I looked at it, it looked like I didn't quite put it in straight. The cat expanded and contracted like a ripe grape to a raisin and a heavy-duty rush came on and it made me do that palsied thing Joe Cocker used to do with his hands. It was so bright in the kitchen and fuckin-A a refrigerator can make a lot of noise. I was still worried that one of the neighbors called the police on me for being naked in my backyard and they just hadn't gotten around to dispatching a car yet. I went and checked the locks on both doors a second time and turned the lights out and as I tiptoed back through the kitchen, a dark figure passed on the stairs and I froze and my mouth went dry until I realized it was my reflection in the hallway mirror. I got right up in front of the mirror, but I didn't look like myself at all anymore; or like it was me, but I just didn't recognize myself. The person in the mirror looked thinner, younger. And I felt a golfball in my throat when I realized I was staring at my older brother. He got killed in a car wreck when he was eighteen and I was seventeen and looking into his dark young eyes, I felt so little in front of him, so average. I never became a successful athlete and I was a fuckup in school and I'll be pissing away my days at the Water Company until I draw a pension like everyone else. And I wished I just had some fucking children to show for it, something so that I could say to him, look there's still hope, *I didn't let you down...*

The mirror shimmied and my eyes got used to the dark and I let out a sigh when I realized it was just me.

God, I felt twitchy all over and my brain felt like it was on double power and I wanted it to stop. I manually set the cable box on the Comedy channel before turning the TV back on. It was the end of a *Saturday Night Live* re-run. Then they played a commercial for a fruit drink with the white guy from *Beverly Hills Cop* and *Fast Times at Ridgemont High* and the fruit was exploding all over the place in a kaleidoscope and the guy rose out of water, but like on the underside and I felt a rush and had to look away until *Saturday Night Live* came back on. Back when I was in high school, once 11:30 rolled around, the music was turned off and everyone, zonked out of their brains, jockeyed for spots around the TV like Indians around the campfire. They played that sketch of Dan Akroyd doing Jimmy Carter, except Carter knew all about drugs and he was counseling this one kid over the phone who took too much acid and Jesus Christ, I thought, somebody is definitely watching me. Anyway, I remembered the stinger from high school when Carter told the kid to drink a beer and listen to school when Carter told the kid to drink a beer and listen to the Allman Brothers. But the thing was, at that very moment, there was this kid upstairs who was freaking out on acid and one guy said why don't we pipe the Allmans into the kid's room just for a goof—we knew they did tons of drugs on SNL and so we did it and the kid actually started to get his shit together and groove to the Allmans.

I pressed mute and dug out my old LP's and sure enough I had the Best of the Allmans. I dropped the needle all over the edge of the record but then it got going and all these dated guitar and keyboard solos spun out of the speakers, and I closed my eyes to the sound of *Jessica*. The backs of my eyelids were like a movie screen and green ladders spiraled out and the music came to the end of a section and dropped an octave or something and then the ladders turned blue. I stood and flipped off the TV and stretched out on the carpet in the dark. When I closed my eyes again, the ladders came back and I sort of gave in to the twitching all over my body. I got my shit back together and my mind stopped clicking and racing and I thought about my wife and how much I love her and how we got a house and secure jobs and really, I don't got it so bad. Not so bad at all. Yellow starbursts exploded like roman candles between the spiraling ladders and I thought about the Water Commission and how they could all kiss my ass as I watched my own fireworks on the for-real Fourth of July. I drew in a deep breath and let it out.

Schlong of Solomon

I completed my M.A. in comparative literature years ago, but I never went on for my Ph.D. People often wonder why, with my education, I choose to dole out audio and video equipment in the foreign language lounge at Gample University. I tell them with a quick smile that I *enjoy* doing this, and people walk away rather enchanted. By running the language lounge, I remain in a rich cultural milieu, without having to actually teach or deal with the pressure to publish obscure research that no one ever reads.

I must admit, however, that to a certain extent, I am kidding myself; I *dream* about being a professor. I've delivered seventy-five minute lectures on Stendhal to my bathroom mirror. But the "publish or perish" pressure of the academic world is very real, not to mention hacking the political side of becoming tenured. Academics is a bloodsport. Last year, one of the professors in Modern Languages—after being accused of sexual harassment—had to resort to playing the race card to finally scare the committee into approving his tenure. I doubt I could stomach such tactics. Besides, God never informed me of a doctorate in my future; patience is crucial and I simply have to wait for the next instructions. Oh, but I do fancy how the young women look up to the professors! I don't think anything entices me so much as to be admired for one's intellect. Unfortunately, I have to subsist on the casual banter of the language lounge. But most of the part-time help sent over to the lounge by Student Labor are girls. And they're often exceptionally attractive. I attributed the higher frequency of girls to the subconscious sexist ego, compounded by the simple fact that fewer men study foreign languages. Especially French. And most of the men who study French are homosexual abominations anyway. But as for why the girls were so attractive, I can only attribute to God rewarding one of His chosen followers.

Seven years ago, Student Labor sent over a girl to work in the lab; she dressed on the trashy side and proved a constant flirt. One day, I was setting the alarm on my computer desktop and I jokingly handed her the microphone. She grabbed it and hissed in her deep slutty voice: "Wake up, David." I noticed myself setting it more often than necessary and it passed as a joke between us, but I could feel my blood rising. I re-recorded her voice and fixed it in a loop so that it played over and over. The end of "David" trailed into the beginning of "Wake" and it sounded like she was moaning. It had a tremendous effect on me.

Obviously I have access to all the audio equipment one would ever need. I've recorded more than a dozen girls; some knowingly and some unknowingly. To get a really good sample for a long session, they have to know they're being recorded. I usually hand them a microphone under the guise of testing an ancient tape recorder. "Put it right against your chin," I instruct them. They hold the mike right beneath their lips and their breath overpowers the mike and this works very well. It's always a trick to get them to say my name though. Sometimes I follow up my instructions with their name: "O*kay*, *Jen*nifer?" I say in a sing-song voice and Jennifer unflinchingly replies, "O*kay*, *Da*vid."

Then there's the unknowing recordings. I changed the phone in the back room years ago; it's mounted on the wall with a three foot cord so that once someone is speaking, they can't go very far. And I always carry a microcassette recorder in my breast pocket, packed with fresh Duracells for 'notes.' More than half of my unknowing recordings consist of conversations with boyfriends where I simply picked up the receiver in the other room and pressed record. Most of the girls are freshmen and their romances tend to be brief. I usually wait for them to wind down—when the relationship is on its last leg and their voices take on a delicious pleading quality. One of my Greatest Hits consists of a dollish blond begging some young man in a hushed whisper, "But *why?* Don't you *want* to see me? Can't I see you *tonight*?" It's delectable. I made a loop of certain excerpts which I often attach at the end of another tape for the finish. All of my sessions take place in the back room of the language lounge, as I've experienced a distinct aphrodisiac in reconstructing the scenes in their original environment.

My wife Virginia and I only have sex once or twice a month. She's quite attractive, but her father is a minister and she's always been rather frigid. We just don't communicate very well on a sexual level. The formality that exists after six years of marriage does not cease to amaze me. But I always reasoned our lower frequency of lovemaking to be more in accordance with God's will. And I came to view my recordings as a lesser evil—something to help me from day to day to maintain the clarity of my devotion and service to Him. Although sometimes, the tapes alone just aren't enough.

Sarah Corbeaux was blond and tall and stood with perfect posture. She hailed from Minnesota and Student Labor sent her to the lounge the first day of classes. Then, I spotted her the following Sunday at the First Congregational Church on campus. She was alone and I followed her out after the service. She seemed to dawdle by the pond, as though admiring the ducks.

"Sarah," I called out.

She spun around displaying a look of desperate optimism. I couldn't tell if she was pleased or not to discover that it was me who recognized her, but I think she was.

"It's quite a leap you made, coming here all the way from Minnesota," I said.

"Yes," she blushed. "I'm the first person in my family to go to college."

"And I'll bet you don't know a soul in the East."

She shook her head 'no' and I detected a moderate case of homesickness. I invited her to a gathering of my Bible group.

"Oh. Ummm..."

"It's mostly young people. I'm about the oldest guy there," I assured her. "We socialize too, you know. It's fun."

"Okay," she said. A flicker of interest.

She attended our meeting and was invited to read aloud a passage from Kings. She ran her index finger down the table of contents and I surmised that she wasn't well acquainted with the Bible. But she commenced reading and her voice took on a huskier, more authoritarian quality, like a young school teacher. My knees began to knock.

Now, usually upon hearing a girl for the first time, I can tell if I want to record her. In my two brief conversations with Sarah, the odd meter of her Minnesota accent failed to inspire me; but when she read...I knew that I had to record that voice.

For weeks, I waited with the patience of Job, but *that* voice never surfaced in the casual banter of the language lounge. Midway through the semester, my patience got the best of me and I led her to the back room and handed her a microphone to test a recorder.

"What do I do?" she asked.

"Just read something."

"What should I read?"

"Ohh, it doesn't matter really," I said, scanning the lounge in a quick half-circle. "I know." I reached for my bag. "Let's get Biblical!" I said with mock enthusiasm, doing that silly celebratory gesture the kids do with their fists.

"Okay," she giggled, taking my Bible from my hands. "In the beginning?"

"No, no. Too heavy." I noticed my hands were shaking as I replaced my bag. "Something lighter. A bit more poetic." I snapped my fingers. "Song of Solomon."

"Is it long?"

"Oh, no, it's quite short," I assured her, my blood pumping upon discovering that she wasn't familiar with that wonderful little book. I tried to steady my twitching fingers as I found the page. I handed her the Bible and she rolled her shoulders back and sat up straight, her wide derrière perched on the lip of the desk, her plaid skirt stretched over her pleated hips, oh God, and I waited for *that* voice. She cleared her throat and began:

> "*Oh that you would kiss me with the*
> *kisses of your mouth!*
> *For your love is better than wine-*"

"Whoa," she cut herself off. "What is this?" She fingered the page and closed the cover to verify that it was in fact the Bible I had handed her.

"You've never read this?" I chided her. "It's a love poem."

"I didn't know there were things like this in the *Bible*," she said.

"It's not just an eye for an eye, you know," I said, trying to laugh. Meanwhile I'm very aware that her mildly shocked reaction is being recorded. Very aware.

"The two lovers are representative of God's love for his chosen followers," I stated matter of factly, nodding at her in a way to let her know that I wholeheartedly considered her to be one of God's chosen; after all, she was of service to me. "It's rather beautiful."

Her eyes skimmed across the text and she recommenced reading, but she drifted back to her normal speaking voice, somewhat hurrying to the end of the chapter.

"You have a powerful voice," I tried. "Do you do any theatre?"

"I did in high school." She rolled her eyes. "I was thinking about going out for a play next semester, but I don't know..."

"You really should. You project quite well."

"Do you think so?"

"Sure. You could do voice-overs. Why don't you keep reading?"

"Okay." She tossed her flaxen mane and re-opened the Bible.

"Try chapter 4," I hastily added.

"Okay. Chapter four." She sat up straight and licked her lips and I admired her exquisite form, wishing I had set up the hidden camcorder instead.

> *"How sweet is your love, my*
> *sister, my bride,*
> *how much better is your love*
> *than wine,*
> *and the fragrance of your oils*

than any spice!
Your lips distill nectar, my bride;
honey and milk are under your
tongue-"

She looked at me and I nodded her on.

"*Who is this that looks forth like the*
the dawn,
fair as the moon, bright as the sun,
terrible as an army with banners?"

I rested my chin on my hand and studied her reading with sheer admiration, of which not an ounce was feigned. She really turned up the theatre during Chapter Seven, using her free hand for gestures and gently rocking on the desk, delivering the lines like a wan seductrice:

"*How graceful are your feet in*
sandals,
O queenly maiden!
Your rounded thighs like jewels,
the work of a master hand.
Your navel is a rounded bowl
that never lacks mixed wine.
Your belly is a heap of wheat,
encircled with lilies.
Your two breasts are like two fawns,
twins of a gazelle.
Your neck is like an ivory tower.
Your eyes are pools in Heshbon,
by the gates of Bathrabbim.
Your nose is like a tower of Lebanon
overlooking Damascus.

Your head crowns you like Carmel,
and your flowing locks are like purple;
a king is held captive in the tresses."

She replaced one of her own tresses behind her ear, exposing her slender neck and I closed my eyes, imagining that she was the lover and I was the maiden.

"How fair and pleasant you are,
O loved one, delectable maiden!

You are stately as a palm tree,
and your breasts are like its clusters.

I say I will climb the palm tree
and lay hold of its branches.
Oh, may your breasts be like clusters of the vine,
and the scent of your breath like apples,
and your kisses like the best wine
that goes down smoothly
gliding over lips and teeth."

My tape came to an end and she put down the microphone. My eyes swam over her tall figure to her wholesome face and I felt a pang in my stomach. Even though the recording would be a real treasure, in the back of my mind, I knew that eventually the tape alone would not be enough. I thanked her and waved my hand at the time cards and then nodded towards the door.

"I'll punch you out," I said, holding my finger over my lips, to imply that it was our little secret, knowing very well that her acceptance of this small infraction would lay the foundation for further impropriety. She grabbed her bag and bid me goodbye.

The black hands crawled at a torturous pace around the large white face of the clock, as I listened to mindless banter about Gample University's men's basketball team and the "Big Game" they were to play that evening. Almost five o'clock; I needed to call Dr. Tartov in Paris. He was one of two male professors in Gample's French department—a real heavy hitter—an alcoholic blowhard—but a man with lots of pull. It seems one of the girls in the lab had complained to one of the female professors about a comment I made regarding the erectness of her nipples. This happens from time to time; Dr. Tartov—or Dr. Tartuffe, as I like to refer to him—speaks with the professor and she invariably backs off. I don't know if he has dirt on everyone or if they're just intimidated by him. Either way, these professors explain to the girl that I'm a family man who is very active in my church and she must have misunderstood a poor attempt at humor that was supposed to pass for an old-school pleasantry. It's good in a way, as the warnings help keep me in check.

The big hand clicked onto the twelve—exactly eleven o'clock in France. As I dialed, I worried that Tartov would already be in his cups. He seemed lucid when he answered, but he talks a great game when he's loaded.

"Don't worry, David," he said in his big-hearted way. "I'll take care of it."

What a guy. The reality of the situation was that he had to help me; at his request, I had intercepted a few early morning faxes sent to the French department from the 24-year-old assistant director of his study-abroad program—a luscious young thing citing "odd behavior" along with questions young thing citing "odd behavior" along with questions about Dr. Tartov's handling of the program's funds. I could just picture Tartuffe over in Paris all by himself with free reign over an expense account and eight young women. Oh how I *wish* I could have gone on for my Ph. D!

Finally it was time to close the lab and I retreated to my office and removed the Tanya cassette—a soft-spoken Korean girl I had recorded earlier that morning—and hastily rewound the Sarah cassette and played it, pressing stop immediately after hearing her voice. Oh God! I wrote her name in Greek letters on the label and phoned Virginia. I told her I would be working late in the language lab and to pick up the kids. I locked the door to the lounge and turned off the lights and went into the lab and twisted the lock and then I stepped into the back room and locked the door with my key from the inside. I rewound the cassette to the beginning and plugged in a set of headphones and eyed the edge of the desk which cradled her wide exquisite buttocks until I could see the outline of her posture. I arranged my necessary items within reach on the desk and unzipped my pants and pressed play.

> *"Oh that you would kiss me with the*
> *kisses of your mouth!"*

That husky growl crackled in my ears, its cooing lilt rising and falling. I adjusted my black lace panties and tightened the extension cord around my neck as I closed my eyes and thanked God for giving me Sarah.

Our National Pastime

This story is dedicated to the memory of Ali Ramirez.

Me and George copped bleacher seats a dollar off from a scalper and crossed the street under the el tracks to throw back a slice and a tall can of beer. It would be nice to go in early and have a beer while watching batting practice, but beer is too expensive inside the Stadium. So I bought another brown-bagged 16 oz. can of Bud before walking out. Georgie burned half a Marlboro in three straight hits and I drained my Bud just as we arrived at the bleacher entrance. They didn't frisk us when we passed through the turnstile and we sat down in front of a clump of high school kids just as they cranked up the familiar Bob Merrill recording of the Star-Spangled Banner. I took off my cap and placed it over my heart, staring out at Old Glory wrapped around the pole like a candy cane over the dead air in Monument Park, while one of the kids in back of me rattled off some bullshit story about getting blown by some chick.

Man, I love being in the Stadium. Steinbrenner's fucking nuts, thinking he's gonna build a new stadium in Jersey. Even though it'd be a lot easier to get to from Lodensack, I'd never go to it. That numbnuts doesn't fucking understand that the whole thing about the Stadium is that this where all the great stuff happened. Home plate is the same exact spot where Babe Ruth stood and made the game what it is today. I mean I lived in Jersey my whole life and I fuckin hate New York, but I'd never want to see the Bombers anywhere but the Bronx. But sometimes I wonder why I even give a fuck at all. I played little league like everybody else, but I mostly struck out. My brother was real good and I tried to be good too, but I just never saw the ball coming.

As soon as the Strike happened last year, I knew there would be no World Series simply because the Yanks were in first place and Don Mattingly was finally going to get his crack at a little October baseball. It's fucked up because he was born on the same exact day and year as my brother: April 20, 1961. Donny was 33 last year when the Strike happened and with his back the way it is, it was really his last shot. But he stood by the players and striked even though he doesn't give a fuck about money. That he sacrificed what was probably his only chance to play in a World Series to stick by the players is nothing short of a modern day sports tragedy.

Except for a small cluster perched over home plate, the upper deck was deserted. A lot of people were still bitching and moaning about how the players and the owners are both too greedy. I don't think the players are greedy. Fuckin-A they're businessmen providing a service and they worked a hell of a lot harder to get to where they are than the owners did. When they fuck up there's a thousand guys ready to fill their spots. And last I checked, America was still a capitalist country and the definition of capitalism is that you get as much as you can.

So all these pansy-ass writers go on about how since it's the National Pastime, it's a sad reflection on who we are as a nation or some kind of crap like that. This one guy was really getting into it but he might as well've been speaking French because I couldn't understand what the fuck he was talking about. You know he's that real dorky looking middle-age guy with the glasses and the Richie Cunningham haircut and the bow-tie. Will somebody. He uses all those fancy words I never even heard before. I put it down after the first paragraph because he made me feel like an idiot or something. I don't know who dorkhead thinks he's writing for because Georgie told me that the average reading level in America is seventh grade. Now, I know I aint a brain surgeon or nothing but I did stick it out in J.C. for a semester—which means my reading level is six years higher than average. So even if we was all *forced* to read his hoity-toity piece most Americans wouldn't even be able to tell you his freaking position. What's his name? You know the guy I'm talking about. Will...something. I don't remember. Either way, dorkhead must have a bowtie tightly strung around his nutsack.

Even though Chicago was like twenty games back, they still nailed the Yanks 9-4 in a replay of Monday night's rained out opener. No way were those sorry asses going to beat us twice in one day. It was pretty fucked up because Jack McDowell, who used to be a White Sock, was pitching for the Yanks and then Dave Righetti, who pitched for the Yanks the last time they were in the Series back in '81, was pitching for Chicago.

Lance Johnson led off for Chicago and flied out to center. Then McDowell served one up to Tim Raines and he belted it twenty feet over my head and the whole bleacher section started chanting at the guy who caught it:

"THROW-IT-BACK!"

"THROW-IT-BACK!"

Thirty seconds later, the guy hummed the ball back onto the field and everyone cheered. I thought that was pretty admirable because only a handful of people ever catch homerun balls—even if it is from an opposing team. But then again he probably would have had a bad night if he didn't throw it back. So then Security comes up and chucks the guy out of the Stadium. I couldn't believe it. That's what you get for loyalty these days.

Third at bat was Frank Thomas. He homered to right. Fuckin-A. Back-to-back dingers. The Sox rallied four runs before we even got up to bat.

"We're eaten alive," one of the kids in back of me said.

Jesus Christ these kids today have no fucking hope or faith.

Righetti stood tall on the mound and even though I hoped we clobbered him, I wanted to see him pitch well, because he's old and they had sent him back down to the minors for a while and now he's back and I can't help it if I liked him when he used to play for us, can I?

Bernie led off and singled to center. Good. Then Leyritz, with that Napoleonic straight leg of his, singled to left and the little fuckers behind me are high-fiving each other. And fuckin-A, with a full count, my man O'Neill homered. 4-3 Chicago and all of a sudden the kids in back of me are die-hard Yankee fans again.

"YAN-KEE BASE-BALL!"

"METS SUCK!"

I always thought there was never more of a waste of time than yelling "METS SUCK!" in Yankee Stadium. It would be more constructive to yell "METS SUCK!" in Shea, but obviously you'd get your ass kicked. I mean aside from the fact that you're just screaming up to the sky, everyone at the Stadium already agrees and knows full well that the Mets *do* suck. Yelling "METS SUCK!" in Yankee Stadium takes about as much balls as yelling "NIGGERS SUCK!" at a Klan rally. I mean you think they would have that all worked out by now. Besides, I'd bet you my left one those kids were cheering their little fucking asses off for the '86 Mets. That's the problem with kids today—no fucking loyalty.

I turned to George but he was hunched over his scorecard. He doesn't like to talk when we're in the ballpark. I mean he says stuff but we don't have like conversations or nothing. He pushes down his golf pencil on every play, studying the game like it's a science project.

Anyways, things were looking up. 4-3, one out, Bernie's on and Mattingly steps up to the plate. *Donny Baseball, baby!* So the crowd started going and it felt like Donny was gonna carry the fucking fire brigade and bury Chicago's four runs, but he lined into a double-play and the inning was suddenly over. Jesus I felt bad for him. His numbers weren't what they used to be. And he wasn't hardly crashing the decks and it would take nothing short of a fucking miracle to get the Yanks to the Series this year and he's older than Christ and really, this is his last shot. I thought about those two whiny little fuckers on the radio who were saying he should retire out of respect. They weren't showing him much respect by talking shit about a guy who gave his heart and soul to New York. That's one of the things I fucking hate about New York. A guy has one bad game and all the sports pages scream how we should get rid of him. I mean cut the guy some slack for Chrissakes. But I have to admit that it aged me to hear that a guy who was only a year older than me was being pushed into retirement. Anyways, Donny'll be the only great Yankee to have never won, let alone played in, a World Series. That's really fucking something. I mean, Joe D. played in like twelve of em. He's got more rings than fingers. But Donny Baseball won't even get a crack at a single ring. That's a goddamned shame, because there have been a lot of great Yankees. And there's something about the Yanks that separates them from every other team. And I'm not saying that just because I like them. I mean, there's tradition. A winning tradition. They made baseball a sport and even though it aint what it used to be, this is still, most certainly, our national pastime.

A Boy Scout troop all decked out in their uniforms filed towards the back of the bleachers. They looked all self-conscious like how I remember from when I was in the Scouts and you had to wear your uniform in public. The kids in back of me started chanting:

"CUB-SCOUTS-SUCK!"

"CUB-SCOUTS-SUCK!"

Some of the Boy Scouts removed their baseball-style scouting hats and they turned towards each other with red faces like they had to go to the bathroom as they slumped to the back of the bleachers. Aside from making me feel old, those kids in back of me were Genuine Fucking Assholes.

We made quick work of the Sox in the second. Then Vellarde brought in Fernandez on a double. With the game tied up at four, Ali stood up and led his famous cheer. Anyone who's been to the bleachers since like 1962 knows Ali. He's this old Latino guy with a wrinkled face like that forest fire Indian. He leads his cheer with a cowbell and sometimes he brings along a broom for when the Yanks might sweep.

Ali's the balls. His cheer lasts like thirty seconds and everyone takes their cue and claps at the right time and he cracks a little grin. I love that freakin guy. The last verse of the cheer combines the clapping with everyone screaming:

"HOHHHHHHH!"

"HOHHHHHHH!"

"HOHHHHHHH!"

"HOHHHHHHH!"

Even I join in for this part and then he gives three short dings and everyone chants the order:

"YAN-KEE BASE-BALL!"

"METS-SUCK!"

"WHITE-SOX-SUCK!" (opposing team)

"MAR-TI-NEZ SUCKS!" (opposing team's right fielder)

"BOX SEATS SUCK!"

"EV-RYBODY SUCKS!"

High fives.

In the top of the third with two men on base, Dave Martinez sent one all the way to the right field upper deck. It was a fucking shot and it started a near riot of porker ten-year-olds falling all over each other seven sections away in a mad dash for the ball. You knew that one wasn't getting thrown back. As Martinez took his victory lap around the bases, the kids in back of me screamed:

"MARTINEZ, YOU *SUCK!*"

"YOU FUCKING *SUCK!*"

"HEY, MARTINEZ, YOU GO BOTH WAYS; MEN *AND* BOYS!"

Seven to fucking four. I looked over at the luxury boxes at some people dressed in suits socializing in the doorway. I couldn't believe that. If I ever got the chance to sit in one of those boxes, you could be goddamned sure I wouldn't be hanging out in the hallway. I'd have my nose pressed to the glass and I'd be chugging beer and scarfing down everything in sight. And speaking of scarfing stuff down, I noticed this other guy who's famous in the world of the cheap seats. His name's Chico and he's round as the planet. He wears his pants up over his belly and his zipper must be close to two feet. He used to walk with one of those canes that has like a platform on it and one time against Boston, there was a line at the bleacher ticket window and Chico came waddling up with his cane and everyone called his name and they let him cut the line. Him and Ali; every fucking game. Shit, I remember when I first sat in the bleachers. It was during the '69 season, after my father got laid off. But somebody got him in at the Water Company that winter, so we went back to the box seats in '70. Anyways, I remember seeing Ali back when I was seven years old. He looks exactly the same. He's like one of those people who always looked old but never ages. And I don't think I've ever been to the bleachers and not seen his wrinkled face. I kind of like knowing that he'll always be there. I've watched Ali and Chico go in a few times and they've always produced a ticket. And once I asked one of the bleacher security people if they ever just let them in for free and she said that both of them always pay for a ticket. Goddamnit, I thought, that's fucking loyalty.

You have to really twist your neck around to see the color playboard from the bleachers. But this makes it easy not to look at the commercials. When my father used to take us to the Stadium, they didn't broadcast commercials between innings. And back then the playboard only had one color: Gold. And that was enough. I have a lot of vivid memories from the ballpark back then. I remember that I first smelt marijuana in Yankee Stadium. Some guy was blowing a joint two rows back and my brother asked my father, "Dad, is that man smoking pot?" My father said yes without taking his eyes off the game. And I realized that I had smelled that smell lots of times before, and it smelled a little like Christmastime in church. I turned and looked at the man. He pinched the joint between his thin lips, squinting as he pulled it away. He drowned a coughing fit with a slug of beer and Bobby Murcer was at the plate and he clapped and my father spun me back around but I could still smell and hear the man over my shoulder:

"Come on, Bobby! Hit duh fuckin bawl!"

I also remember that the Stadium was where first I realized it wasn't hip for a boy to drop his pants down to his ankles to take a leak. I must have been about four and my brother was trusted to take me out to the bathroom. My father used to make us wear these really loud striped shirts that were like three times worse than anything you ever saw on the Brady Bunch. That way, if we ever got lost it would be easier to pick us out in the crowd. So we walked into the bathroom and it smelled like sweat and beer and all these men are on line at the urinals, pulling it out right at my eye level, as big as snakes. Finally I get in front of the urinal and unbuckle my pants and let em drop to my ankles, my little pink ass swaying in the breeze beneath my checkered nightmare of a shirt—because that's what I always did at home. A couple of men laughed it up behind me and I looked up at my brother, shaking it through his zipper in a hurry, looking at me as though if he were standing out in Center with The Mick, he'd still be standing too close to me. I never took a leak like that ever again.

Bottom of the third, Mattingly steps up to the plate for his second at bat. One out, two men on base, and Donny is fuckin due. He grounded to short and bolted to first. He's not that fast and everyone knew he wasn't going to beat the throw, but he ran hard anyway. Christ, I really admire that guy.

"MARTINEZ, YOU *SUCK!*"

"YOU FUCKING *SUCK!* YOU KNOW THAT?"

I was thirsty. I held my breath and asked George if he wanted a beer.

"Not at those prices I don't."

That's what I was hoping he'd say. I walked down and there were only five people on line at the smaller bleacher snack bar. But they must've had Jerry's Fucking Kids working the counter because I ended up watching the entire fourth inning on the screen. What the fuck was taking them so long? You know the people in box seats didn't wait whole innings on lines with only five people. I mean how long does it take to pour a beer or slap a dog on a bun. Fuckin-A, can't they get someone for this job who can deliver the goods?

After I was reminded that a single beer in Yankee Stadium sets you back five-fifty, I decided to bypass the three dollar hot dog. I couldn't afford a second beer and I knew I'd get more bang for my buck alcohol-wise on an empty stomach. I wondered: when I was a boy, was the snack bar food so fucking expensive? You know, in comparison with inflation and all. Because if it was, my father must have been biting his nails down to the bone as we chowed hot dog after hot dog. Either that or he just went all out. Nowadays, it would break my bank to take two boys to Yankee Stadium. First off, I'd have to shell out for three box seats—I wouldn't take my kids to the bleachers anymore than I'd rent a skin flick for them. And then the food...I know Georgie brings peanuts and chips when he takes his boys, but you gotta eat hot dogs at the Stadium—it's practically a birthright. I don't know. I guess it's the kind of thing you budget to do once a season.

Back at my seat I sipped the beer and looked over the box seats and up again at the luxury boxes. A couple of dark suits moved around holding glasses of champagne. What a sorry-assed bunch. Christ if I'd ever wear a tie to the Stadium.

"Look at those dumb fuckers over there, George," I said, pointing over at the luxury boxes. "They're not even watching the game."

"If they're so dumb," George said, "then how come they're sitting in the luxury boxes and we're out here?"

I couldn't believe some of the shit he was telling me. He said those people never paid anything because the luxury boxes are like tax deductible, which means that me and him are paying their way since all those people got hotshot accountants who make sure they don't pay taxes. I thought he was shitting me—telling me that it was us who was paying for their champagne and their air conditioning, while we sit behind the outfield on a seat that doesn't even have a fucking back on it.

"Why do you think your beer costs five-fifty?"

"I don't know," I said.

"So that you can cover those people's caviar."

"That is fucked," I said. "I mean that is *fucking* fucked." It's bad enough we have to foot the bill for all those people getting rich off welfare. I never knew I was picking up the tab for the *wealthy.* That is nothing short of being fucked in the head. "Those dipshits aren't even watching the *fucking game*," I said to George. "And who the fuck eats caviar at Yankee Stadium?"

"Don't get all wound up," Georgie said, returning his attention to his scorecard. "You don't even know the half of it."

I gulped a buck and a quarter's worth of my watery beer, thinking about Our National Pastime.

"You know what I'd love to do?" I said. "It would be my *fucking* dream to drag all those fuckers out by their ties and line em up and just off every last one of em." I took another sip of beer and squinted at home plate. "Goddamnit if *I'm* going to pay for *them*. And then you know what I'd do? I'd snatch up all their plastic and I'd buy enough beer and dogs to feed the entire crowd in the bleachers."

George turned and stared at me like I had eight heads.

"What are you fucking *nuts?!* What the fuck kind of sicko psychotic bullshit are you spewing now?!"

"But it's fucked up, us paying for them. I'm barely getting by and I'm paying for the rich people?"

"Do you realize," he said all serious, "that it is my dream to one day sit in a luxury box at Yankee Stadium?" He looked at me and I looked down. Shit like this happened all the time between us. George was a lot smarter than me. And lots of times even though I still thought I was right, I just didn't know what to say. I wish I never dropped out of J.C. George looked back down at his scorecard and I raised my yellow paper cup, but it was empty. Maybe I am crazy, I thought, working the whole thing over in my head. Like I said, I aint no brain surgeon, but I was certain of two things: I was paying to sit in the bleachers and I wouldn't ever sit in one of them luxury boxes. And the people in the luxury boxes weren't paying anything. I felt my pocket and my billfold was still there. I burped and crumpled my cup and without saying anything, I got up and went back to the snack bar. I bought a second beer *and* a hot dog, even though it costed eight-fifty, because that's what you're *supposed* to eat at the Stadium. I loaded the dog up with golden mustard and bit into that juicy frank and mustard got stuck on the corners of my mouth and I chewed twice then filled my mouth with beer and I swished it all around with the half-chewed dog and swallowed it and it was fucking delicious.

It was still seven-four Chicago going into the fifth. Righetti was sending solid pitches over the plate and then I realized we were getting clobbered by *two* former Yankees in a row, as Jim Abbot literally single-handedly beat us in game one. Not only that; Rags and Abbot were the last two

Yankees to have pitched no-hitters since Don Larsen's perfect game in the '56 Series. Abbot got his in '93 and I remember Rags' no hitter back in '83, because it was on the Fourth of July and his last strikeout was against Wade Boggs, who of course now plays for the Yankees. Twelve years and two weeks later and Rags is back up on the mound pitching for Chicago. I really used to like him.

Meanwhile, McDowell was pitching like crap. Martinez singled, then Martin singled, putting Martinez on third, then McDowell, who we paid like four million bucks for, let off a wild pitch and Martinez sailed home and Martin advanced to third. Somebody grounded out, bringing in Martin—nine-four Chicago—way to go, Jack. I don't know what the hell was taking Showalter so long—he's a good coach but he fucking takes forever to yank a pitcher. Guillen flied out and then Lance Johnson singled to center. When Showalter headed out to the mound, he practically got an ovation. Some fans booed McDowell as he walked off and Jack gave them the finger. And that fucking cocksucker didn't just flip the bird—he twirled it in a circle, waving it at the entire Stadium. I twisted in my seat because I wanted to see it on the color playboard, but they covered it up with a Budweiser ad.

What the fucking fuck. I mean the guy played like crap and we let him know about it. Maybe these guys do make too much money. As Jack neared the dugout, I realized he was wearing Rags' old number 19 and really, even though Rags was pitching for Chicago, he was more of a Yankee than McDowell could ever hope to be. McDowell was just another seven-figure free agent—a fucking soldier-for-hire who choked against his former teammates. He was hardly justifying all the money Steinbrenner was paying him and that's the only reason he was wearing pinstripes to begin with. Fucking mercenary. Donny played his entire career in New York while he probably could have been paid more to play for a Series contender. But he stuck around. That's fucking loyalty. Not like this asshole. Christ I must be fucking nuts paying cash to come all the way out here. Steinbrenner'd be lucky if there were 20,000 people out here tonight. They should be kissing *our* asses and this fucker's got the balls to flip us off. Fuckin-A this sport's going down the drain. My father had guys like Whitey Ford up on the mound and I get stuck with an ungrateful multi-million dollar fuckup *flipping me off*. The kids in back of me booed McDowell too, but watch—Jack *is* good—and when he bounces back those little snot rags'll be the first in line sucking him off. Christ. Joe D., *he* was class. Simon and Garfunkel were right. And then when The Mick took over, every boy worshiped him. Those guys roamed centerfield like fucking panthers or gods or something. My father once met Mickey Mantle in a restaurant about twenty years ago and The Mick signed out a ball with my brother's name on it and I still got it at home and if you met my father, even though he's not all there any more, he'll still fit in somehow about how he once shook hands with Mickey Mantle. Except for Donny Baseball, the Mick's my favorite player of all-time. But it *is* kind of fucked that after boozing it up all his life he gets a new liver, when some poor kid out there—who through no fault of his own—is going to die because Mickey Mantle bumped him in line for a liver.

The Yanks couldn't get anything going in the fifth and with two outs Donny stepped up to the plate and brought the inning to an end. This fat guy with a Chicago hat, stood with his forearms hanging over the railing of the second tier. The kids in back of me flipped him off and then everyone started chanting "ASS-HOLE! ASS-HOLE!" to the tune of AIR-BALL! and a big smile stretched across the guy's face and even though everyone was calling him a homo and all, he was clearly enjoying himself. He stepped away after he had his fill, leaving the kids standing on their seats. A little girl with a Yankee hat appeared near the railing and the kids started chanting JUMP! JUMP! JUMP! JUMP! until she disappeared and when no one was left, they cued up and chanted:

"BOX SEATS SUCK!"

"BOX SEATS SUCK!"

"YOU PAID NINE-TEEN, WE PAID SIX!"

"WE ARE COOL AND YOU SUCK DICKS!"

Righetti got an ovation from the box seats when he left in the sixth and I stood and clapped for him while the kids in back of me booed.

"YAN-KEE BASE-BALL!

"METS SUCK!"

"RIGHETTI SUCKS!"

Christ, these kids. One of them had a wad of straw duct-taped to his hat which was supposed to be like, we want Strawberry. I couldn't believe these fucking kids yelling Mets suck yet dying to see that fucking unrepentant wife-beater drug-addict, tax-evader in pinstripes. Strawberry was like *the* Met, and now these kids want him to play for the Yankees.

In the middle of the seventh they asked us to rise while they played a recording of "Take Me Out to the Ballgame." I didn't get up. The kids in back of me sang along with their own fucked up lyrics:

"BUY ME SOME HEROIN AND SMOKE SOME CRACK..."

Fucking God help us.

A few rows over I could hear Chico talking with someone but they were speaking Spanish and the only thing I understood was the players names. Chico was wearing a beatup number 7 T-shirt and I thought about The Mick and how he might die and then I looked up at the luxury boxes again and I said a prayer for him. The kids in back of me talked more bullshit and they were most certainly fucked and I thought about how I probably wouldn't ever have any kids of my own, and I changed my prayer so that The Mick would fully recover and come play in the old-timers game and then down an entire case of Jack and just abuse the shit out of his new liver until it was shot and then get another and another and another. Fuck the children.

Nine-four Chicago.

Donny popped out and brought the seventh to a close. A hitless night for Donny Baseball.

"He fucking sucks!" one of the kids grumbled.

People started to file out of the park and I looked over at Chico and his arms were folded and his droopy cheeks were sliding off his face. Ali studied the game a few rows behind me as though we were in extra innings.

"Let's get the fuck out of here," George said, crumpling up his scorecard.

"Did you get a warning yet?" I asked him, not looking at him.

"No," he said, squeezing the scorecard into a ball in his palm.

"Then light up. They don't care."

"Yeah..." George shrugged. Thirty seconds later he moved in back of me and lit up, holding the Marlboro down between his ankles. I didn't say anything. I just sat there and wished it would rain. I wished the sky would burst and start raining cats and dogs until the game was called and the entire field was flooded. And I wished it would drown McDowell and Steinbrenner and that tight-assed dorkhead columnist and the kids in back of me. I don't know why but I started thinking about my brother and the crackup that killed him right after he got recruited. As hard as I try, I can't fully focus in on his face, but I always imagine how he would have turned out real nice and all and I always think about how I should try and be like how he never got a chance, even though I know it could never happen. But I really wish I never dropped out of J.C.

The ChiSox batted in another two runs in the eighth—fuck it—I don't care to get into it. People started pouring through the aisles like Jews through the Red Sea. The kids in back of me were long gone and I looked over at Monument Park at the retired numbers on the Wall. I'd like to go down there some time, but they don't let in the people who sit in the bleachers. I guess they're worried we'd go sit in the empty box seats. I could picture Donnie's 23 just to the right of Reggie's 44. Fucking Steinbrenner better put his number up there. Shit, if he doesn't, I'll never ever set foot in Yankee Stadium ever again. And that's the God-honest fucking truth. Even though Donny probably won't ever get a crack at the Series, in some ways, he's greater than the rest of the retired numbers.

I walked up to the front of the bleachers and hung my arms over the railing. The Stadium was calm, like an empty church, or an ocean the morning after a storm. I looked over the outfield under the lights and even though the white pinstripes were soiled and the infield was pretty torn up, I still admired the overall neatly groomed element of the whole thing. I mean, I *love* the Yankees—even if they are fucked—I could never place my loyalty with another team. All I can do is hope for the best.

For some reason, I remembered the last game of a three-game series with Boston. The Yanks swept and Ali was there with his broom and he led the whole bleacher section out after the game, everyone following him like he was the fucking Pied Piper, as he dinged his bell and we all yelled "*NINE*TEEN-*EIGHT*EEN!" right at the Boston fans who came to the game, rubbing that long lost year of their last World Series championship in their faces. And I don't think I'd ever seen Ali so happy as when we swept Boston. I mean the guy was beaming with joy. And I know it sounds corny or whatever, but it made me happy to see a guy who's so devoted to a team get a little something back. Because sometimes I worry that fifty years from now Boston fans'll be chanting "1978" about us. Believe me, I'm not holding my breath until they win the Series again—I'd just like to follow Ali out of the bleachers like that one last time.

The fucking Chicago White Sox swept the Yanks in the double-header with two former Yankees on the mound. As I turned to go, I caught a glimpse at the little board that broadcasts the scores from the other games and my knees buckled. The fucking Mets pounded the Cubs 12-3.

"When's Boston going to be in town next?" George asked me.

"I don't know," I said, too lazy to unfold the schedule in my shirt pocket.

"Do you want to go?"

"Yeah, sure," I said, gazing over at Ali as he zipped up his navy blue team jacket.

M—ville

Note: This story originally shared the title of a popular song by Jimmy Buffett. However, Coral Reefer Publishing denied a permissions request to reprint the chorus from this song; they felt that the inclusion of the lyrics in this story would be unbecoming to the song's image. Coral Reefer also forbade any reference to the song, or mention of a restaurant that bears the song's name. As per their demand, the lyrics were removed from the story, and any mention of Mr. Buffett's song title has been abridged.

I put on my favorite Calvins that I've had since I was like fifteen and when I got them they were way big on me and even though I haven't really grown since then, the jeans shrank some and I guess I'm a little bigger. They're really tight but I get away with it and they make my butt look really good. But I knew I had to be totally careful because so many girls go away to college and just blow up. I lay back on my bed and lifted my legs in the air to slide them on. Then I stood up on tippy toes and breathed in to zip them up.

My date is so cute and he looks just like Jason Priestly, but it's totally weird because like his name actually *is* Brandon and he has the exact same haircut and people tell him all the time that he looks like him, except he's not *that* cute and he's a little chubbier. He's got the tiniest double chin just like my dad's and his eyebrows are perfect and when I asked him if he tweezed he looked *really* upset. I mean, like, I was just trying to make conversation because I was like, so totally in love with him.

And what's really funny is that I actually watched *Beverly Hills* as I put on my makeup. It's my total favorite show. I used to watch it with my friends in high school and I remember thinking like maybe it might not be cool to still watch it in college, like maybe they would think I was a baby, but all the girls in the sorority I'm pledging still watch it. I couldn't believe it. Except when they watch it, they just totally make fun of it and say how stupid it is. So if other people are there I just like scoff at it too. What's so weird about *90210* is it's so totally unreal. Like they do so many things that never ever happen. But there's also so many things they totally *don't* do that really do happen. Like how they make a big deal about having sex the first time, when we all lost our virginity like years ago and it totally wasn't a big deal at all.

When I told my big sister that I was going out with Brandon, she was like, Alicia, you better be careful because he dates a lot of girls. I was like, Oh my God. Are you my mother? So I was like yeah, totally and I was cool about it because you know she's just totally jealous because she would love to go on a date with him and he asked me out only a month after I arrived at Gample.

I sat by my window and watched the cows as I waited for Brandon to arrive. My dorm is the total last building in the middle of East Buttfuck. But it's across the street from the dairy farm, and my room is on the end so at least I have a great view. Sometimes, I can sit and watch the cows for hours, the way other people watch fish. What's so totally weird about the cows at Gample is that they've got a whole field to hang out in, but they all crowd into the same little spot.

Sometimes there's one like, loser cow standing away by himself, but usually, what happens is one of the cows will start to move away, but not really leave the pack, and the rest of them follow and they all just sort of shift from place to place. During parents' weekend, my dad totally made fun of me when I told him I like to watch the cows. But he watches like, racecar racing, which is totally just cars going around in a circle, so whatever.

Brandon finally came and he wore a white polo shirt and he looked really clean and we walked down to his car and drove along these empty country roads to this bar and restaurant called M—ville. There was like, a bouncer at the door and I told Brandon I didn't have an ID, and I felt really stupid because I wasn't old enough and he said "Don't worry," like I should just shut the fuck up and be cool, and I *totally* did.

"Take out your license," Brandon said.

I did and we got to the bouncer and Brandon said hi and looked at the bouncer and the bouncer took my license that says that I was only born in 1977 and he looked at me and I swallowed loud enough that you could like, hear it, but the bouncer said okay.

We walked under one of those big things with like, vines and roses on it, and stepped through the swinging doors that are like doors in the old west. There was a fire in the back and M—ville was like a cross between an old west saloon and a ski lodge. We sat down and he asked me if I liked margaritas, don't I?

"Of course," I said, even though I never had one before. He ordered a quart and it was white and foamy and came really fast in one of those glass bottles that milk came in when like, my father was little. He poured me a glass and I took a sip and it wasn't too, too bad.

"I can hardly taste the alcohol," I said.

"I know," he said and I took another sip and like it tasted totally good. He finished his glass and poured himself another. I still had most of mine left.

"Paging nurse Alicia. Paging nurse Alicia," he said, like it was coming out of a P.A. "You're wanted at the front desk for another drink."

"Okay." I laughed. He's really funny. I finished my glass really quick and it gave me a headache like when I swallowed too much ice cream when I was little. He refilled my glass to the top.

"That was so totally cool how you got me in," I said.

"I know the guy," he said. "He's one of my Brothers."

Drinking margaritas was so much better than drinking beer. God, I *really* hate beer. It's like, ughhh, but after three or four I don't seem to mind the taste. I couldn't believe it when he told me margaritas were made with tequila. Once I did a shot of tequila and it was totally gross. We finished our pitcher and Brandon ordered another one along with two shots of tequila. Oh well.

They give you these like, free nachos and they're really salty and they just keep bringing out more and more salsa and the salsa's pretty spicy and I ate a bunch of them because dinner in the dorm was like, gross, but you have to be totally careful eating things like nachos on a date because it's so easy to spill and you'll look like a total dweeb. I finished my glass and the song, M—ville came on and like, this woman behind the bar started like dancing and shaking as she poured a drink and I was like, wouldn't they be really sick of this song, working in a restaurant with the same name? I mean they must hear it at least twice a night.

"I guess they just get used to it," Brandon said, looking at a group of people in the corner. He started like, singing the chorus without really making any noise, but he cut himself off on the last line to sip his drink.

The new pitcher came with these like mongo tequila shots and little slices of lime that were *so* cute. Brandon licked his hand near his thumb and covered it with salt and grabbed the lime and then the tequila with the other hand and like, now I was more worried that I would screw up holding all of those things and I'd look totally stupid.

I must have looked really nervous because he like, leaned over and said, "Just open your mouth and swallow the whole thing, okay? One, two, THREE."

I licked the salt and opened my throat and swallowed the shot and then sucked hard on the lime and like, it was totally gross, but I guess I could see how you could get into it.

Ten minutes later we were halfway done with the second quart and like, I was feeling totally fucked up. Like, I was talking and he just kept grinning at me and it was so weird because like, words were just coming out of my mouth and like, part of me was just watching myself talk and some of the things I started to say were like, totally stupid, but Brandon just kept grinning and waving to some guys he knew and filling up my glass and like, I don't know, I just didn't want him to think I was like a total idiot.

I looked over at the fire and then my head started to like, you know, when you're like *too* fucked up? And I had to like, hold on to the edge of the table as guys he knew kept coming by, but I was cool. Then I looked over at the corner of the bar and a waitress was refilling the salsa bowls. The empties all had a little salsa left in the bottom and like, salsa dripped over the side from a bunch of drunk people dipping their chips in them and I thought that must be like, so totally gross on the bottom with like everyone's chip backwash. But like the waitress? She picks up one of the little bowls and instead of washing it out and refilling it, she just like takes one of the little cocktail napkins and like, I can see the M—ville logo on it and she just wipes off the sides of the bowl and fills it to the top with more salsa. I was like, Ugh! That is *so* fucking rude! It made me like, gag and I got up to go to the bathroom and I'm glad it was really crowded because I don't think I was like, walking right and it felt like everyone was watching me—but like I can't walk right even when I'm sober if I know people are watching me.

There was a line at the bathroom but like, I totally couldn't deal with standing there and like I couldn't stop touching my face. I finally got inside and turned on the cold and filled my mouth with cold water and swallowed and it tasted so good and it cleaned out that like pre-puke taste you get in the back of your throat and I felt better in the like, quietness of the bathroom and I was totally glad I didn't puke because your breath stinks and like you can totally tell and it would have destroyed our first date.

I think I was still walking a little funny. And when I got back to the table, he asked me if I blew.

I was like, *No*.

And he was like, That's good. Why don't I take you home?

And I was like, Okay, like I didn't care, even though I totally couldn't deal with M—ville anymore.

He walked in front of me and I followed him through the old west doors and under that like gate-thing with the flowers and vines and then he stopped outside and turned around and waited for me. It felt so good to be outside in the cool air. I danced in a little circle because I was so psyched to finally be at Gample on my own. I had been counting the days since like, the beginning of junior year and it seemed like I would never get to college, but it finally came and now I can do whatever I want without my parents being like, Where are you *going,* Leash? When will you be *home,* Leash? Leash? *Leash?* God I love the dorm it's like, so cool and like my room's perfect and like the two best sororities gave me bids and Brandon opened my door with the key and then held open the door for me and helped me in and then closed my door and I was really touched by like, how polite he was and I leaned over to kiss him, but he stopped me and was like, Just wait. He drove really fast around turns and like the ride home made me like, woozy. I almost felt like I was going to puke, but not really. I sort of remember him taking me up to my room and like, I sat on the floor in the hallway while he grabbed my keys and like, jammed them in the door until he found the right one.

I woke up at seven o'clock and when I sat up I was so hung over I could have like, cried. My Calvins were tangled up with my underwear around my ankles and my chest was like totally out of my bra. I guess he tried to help me undress, but like, couldn't deal with my shoes. I looked over on my nightstand and there was a piece of paper that said, I'LL CALL YOU. I was like, oh, God, I hope I didn't like do anything stupid last night—I was so wasted—I hope I didn't like say stupid stuff—I hope he calls today oh God, I felt like shit and my butt felt sticky and I remembered the salsa and oh no I didn't—I reached down, but like, I guess I just got really sweaty from sleeping in my clothes. I pulled up my Calvins, but I didn't even try to zip them up and I grabbed my stuff for the shower and went to the bathroom. I was still like, walking funny, and the bathroom was empty except for this one really slutty senior girl at the far sink. She turned and looked at me and I looked at myself in the mirror and my makeup was all smeared and I looked like total shit and I could see her staring at me in the mirror and suddenly, I remembered that she was there last night when Brandon was trying to get the key into my door and like, she said something to him like I was a baby and I was drunk and like I totally told her to just shut the fuck up and like I just remembered the whole thing. She was still staring at me in the mirror and I looked back at her like, what the fuck are you staring at, and she looked away. She's a total fucking slut. She's been with like half the guys on the floor below and when she's done, she like hangs the condom up on her wall.

I went into a stall and sat down. After I heard her leave, I stood up and I didn't even have to use my finger. I can make myself puke with a trick I learned from my older sister when I was like twelve. I still felt like shit but like I totally felt better. My butt still felt weird like I had to go but not really. I flushed and sat back down and a little came out and it burned. It must have been all of that spicy salsa. When I stood up, there was like blood in the toilet and it totally freaked me out and I flushed it and got right in the shower and some pink water ran down my leg and down the drain. I started to get light-headed and I made the shower colder and I kept making it colder until it was like almost totally cold and like I didn't even care. It felt good and I let my mouth fill up with water and swallowed a bunch of times before I turned it off. I still felt a little woozy and I went back to my room and I took half of a valium that I save for special occasions and I had a nine o'clock in the Math and Science Building and I was like, *yah*, I'll definitely be borrowing the notes for that one. I laid down in bed and closed my eyes until I couldn't feel anything.

I woke up at 11:30 and I felt totally better. I had a dream—or like, I wasn't really sure if I just dreamt it, or if I was remembering an old dream or something from a long time ago. But I was little and I was in the bathtub with my sister and my father and I was sitting in front of him and he was shampooing my hair and my mom was drying off my sister and I could like, feel my father behind me. My mom was looking right at me, but she couldn't see anything, and like, I wasn't able to talk. Whatever. I got dressed and the dairy farm was like, totally deserted. It looked cold outside and I guess the cows were in the barn thing.

I went down to the cafeteria for a salad. It was early and there was this totally dorky group of people there, but I didn't really know anyone else and I hate standing there holding a tray, so I sat down by myself. But like, two seconds later, this girl that I know walked by and I said hi and like she totally stared at me but didn't say anything? I was like, fuck *you*, you're a total bitch. I thought about Kappa Kappa Gamma's party later on and like, I totally had to just continue making a good impression on them. I wasn't really hungry and I threw out the salad and went up to my room and I turned on the TV to my third favorite soap and I put on my makeup and called my big sister and she was like, how was your date with Brandon? And I was like, it was totally cool and she was like, whoa. And I was like, I'm really excited for tonight. And she was like, yeah, everyone totally likes you. I got off the phone with her and did my eyes. And in the mirror I could see the little note Brandon left and I looked over at the phone and I was like, I totally hope he calls me soon.

Pls. Allow 4-6 Wks for Armageddon

I flipped off the Mr. Coffee and crashed down in front of CNN while thumbing through the *New York Times*, looking for signs that the world was coming to an end. The way things are heating up, it can't possibly be that far off. And you know CNN'll be broadcasting live right up to the Final Hour. It'll be a helluva lot better than any of the bullshit on TV nowadays. And goddamnit, I just can't wait to see it when the whole shithouse goes up in flames. I think I've got a pretty good shot. I'm 69. But I still manage 40 pushups every morning and longevity runs in my family. I've got a solid twenty years left and I don't see how the world could possibly outlive me. Although I have to admit, this isn't the first time I thought we were at the Beginning of the End. After Truman dropped the big one on the Japs, I thought it was just a matter of time before the Rooskies farted and we blew each other to Kingdom Come. But when the Cuban Missile Crisis blew over, I figured that was as close as we'd get. In the latter part of the sixties, I didn't so much think the world was coming to an end, but I sure as hell thought the U.S. was on its last leg. Shit; the Romans had their day—I figured this was ours. Everyone and their brother was gettin picked off like flies and all those goddamned kids zapped outta their heads—I just figured if we somehow got past the assassinations and the burning riots, that all the hippies couldn't possibly raise normal kids—and they didn't—that generation's even more in the toilet than they were—but here we are.

Sure, some people think I'm nuts. But ask those same people if they think the United States will last forever. They're speechless. *Nothing* lasts forever. Am I nuts for believing that? Well nowadays, I have a lot more faith in the United States. We will last forever—that is to say our demise will coincide with the demise of Mankind. During the Cold War, it was at least plausible that if America fell, the Rooskies would take our place. But if America fell today, the world would tailspin in a power struggle—anarchy would be the lunch special across the map. Boy, that would be something to see. When I try to picture it, all I see is smog and garbage. Like in that Charlton Heston picture where it takes that numbnuts forever to figure out that the crackers were made of dead people. And I'll bet there'll be rats, too. Rats as big as cats running wild. I once read this article in *National Geographic* about rats. If you put a male and a female together in one room, six months later you'll have seven thousand. They can eat anything—with teeth that can cut through steel pipes. They can fall five stories and dust themselves off and walk away. They can fit through a hole the size of a quarter and can tread water for two days straight. Not to mention being able to absorb levels of radiation beyond a nuclear explosion. Do you want to hear about cockroaches? You're talking two tough species—species that will certainly outlive Man. But rats and roaches'll make a healthy balance. The rats'll be like the capitalists and the cockroaches like the commies.

Ever wonder how the Last Man will die? I've been through just about all the possible scenarios. And I'd have to place my money on him being overtaken by a pack of cat-sized rats as God licks his finger and turns a page.

Yes, the United States of America will be Mankind's last empire. It's no secret that we're in our decline. Yet who could come close to bringing America to her knees? Maybe, if it was the whole rest of the world vs. us. *Maybe*. But they'd never be able to coordinate it. Too many countries hate each other. And they'd all be yappin in 97 different languages at the same time, trying to figure it out. Our demise will come from within. The next and last big war will begin within our own borders. And I mean a *real* war—not one of these candy-ass Desert Storm bullshits. Hell, when the militia people blew out that building in Oklahoma? Christ, I was glued to the set, trying to guess what they'd hit next. If there was some way to team them up with the gangs...that would be a helluva card. They've both got enough guns to do it. Hot damn! The *Times* had an article about a string of prison riots. Boy, I wonder if we got more people in prison in America than there are enlisted in the Armed Forces.

But if Man could make it past the Fall of America, we still wouldn't last as a species. Unlike the dinosaurs, however, we shall be the masters of our own demise. I read not too long ago that my grandson is only half the man I am. That's right. Men like me who came of age before The War had an average sperm count that is over twice as high as young men today—a mere two generations later. That was back before the Bomb and nuclear energy and before everyone had their own radiation generator spinning their dietetic frozen pizzas in circles. Now obviously if Man could no longer procreate, that would by definition be the end of us. But that would take more than a hundred years. And even if I could make it that long, that would be a really anti-climactic finish to it all. Damnit, I want fire and brimstone. Anyway, they can *already* freeze sperm. I guess that would be kind of comical, though—every healthy young man commissioned to live out his days jacking off into an ice cube tray. But I don't want less, I want more. They got countries in Africa with birth rates so high that the population doubles every eighteen years. And they're not even Catlicks. I wonder what the birth rate is in this country for the blacks and the Puerto Ricans. Christ they fuck like rabbits. I remember reading that by the year 2050, blacks will outnumber whites in America. Now that would certainly make for a more evenly balanced race riot, but again, I know I'm not going to make it that long. Plus AIDS fucks it all up. CNN said that one out of every 150 people in New York City is already HIV positive. It's one in ten in some of those same rundown African nations with the promising birth rates, which means that unless the disease mutates so that you can get it from a cold, AIDS is just going to prolong everything by slowing down overpopulation.

A lot of it's going to be pure chance. A thousand precise elements coming together under specific conditions—like what creates a tornado. But maybe it doesn't have to be so complicated. If an uprising in America could somehow coincide with an environmental disaster, that might be enough. The rainforests seem to be my best hope. I can't remember how many thousand acres get cleared every second, but it's pretty impressive. Hell, with all the McDonald's I've eaten over the years, I could probably take credit for half a South American forest all by myself. It's too bad Mankind won't leave a tombstone for whatever comes after us—all they'll have are the signs at McDonald's proclaiming how many billion hamburgers we've eaten. Boy that'll be a mindfucker. So anyways, with global warming and the rainforests, maybe one day there won't be enough air with too many people to breathe it. The CNN newscaster just mentioned the heat wave that hit Chicago. 500 people dropped dead—a bunch of old people and asthmatics and other weaker breathers and they were telling em not to exert themselves and whatnot. They issued an "ozone warning." I got a kick out of that one—none of the scientists had the balls to admit that it was just plain too hot and not enough air to breathe. Shit, that could be the formula right there! If it gets a little hotter every summer, one day a massive heat wave will hit New York City and all the weaker breathers'll drop dead and soon everyone's feeling a little short of breath and 11 million people break out in a mad dash clawing and climbing over each other to get to the oxygen. All those Wall Streeters would drop their game of charades, or whatever it is they're doing on the trading floor over there and dash off into gridlock trying to get to their summer houses in the Hamptons. The financial center of the world would be left unattended and Hoooweeee!—think of what it would do to the Japs half a world away on their own crowded little island!

But I try not to get too excited. Through the window I saw my daughter's car pull up. She was dropping off my grandson with me for the afternoon. Boy, I love him—never had any boys of my own. I opened the front door and he bolted out of the car. As he ran around the walkway, I could almost see him coming around third base—I can't wait. I caught him in my arms and held him up to the sun and his mother waved and drove off. Back inside CNN's *Earth Matters* had someone going on about learning to recycle plastic. See that's why I try not to get too worked up. Just when things are looking up, something else fucks it up. Sometimes I wonder why I give a rat's ass hoping for it at all. I pressed the red button and looked down upon my smiling grandson.

Interlude

How Many More Miles

The sun inched over the rotting billboard, spilling through the tight window onto the broad expanse of Jesse's back. He squinted and carried the two, calculating in the margin of the TV Guide, the number of Marlboro Miles he still required to obtain the sheepskin Timber Mountain Pullover.

"Only 85 more miles to go," he said to himself. "Shit, that's not even two cartons." He extracted the foil insert of a virgin pack and raised the jaunty filters to the bridge of his cleft frenulum, breathing in the fresh quinoline scent. With the tip of his tongue, he maneuvered one of the filters, wedging it into the gap in his front teeth before retracting the pack. His head pained him more than most mornings, the throb arcing from his temples through the back of his cranium. He rose from the table and turned to his medicine cabinet. Inside, an empty bottle of aspirin stood at attention like a dashboard Jesus for the last six months. He cursed and slammed the door shut, but an ancient NyQuillian crud had affixed the bottle to its spot. Nevertheless, these repeated visits to his sparse medicine cabinet had proven adequate, as four months had passed since Jesse had ingested the last four aspirin. He sat back down and reached for his monogrammed Marlboro zippo. Through the coarse skin on his thumb, he could barely perceive the spin wheel as the flint sparked and the tip of his cigarette came to life. He inhaled the dank blue flame with his first hit of the day, rising from the table to gather the empty cans of Genesee that adorned his living quarters from the previous night's soiree. But the residue from the spilled cream ale adhered his foot to the floor, bringing up the corner of the cracked, bubbled linoleum with his first step.

Jesse shook his head in disgust upon marking the beaded condensation beneath the rim of an opened can. What a waste, he thought, feeling the heft of the can and the cramp that persisted in his lower back from too much overtime at the garage.

"If only they left me one can" he lamented, "just to start off my day..." The can still felt a tad cold and he blew off the single deposit of cigarette ash from the rim and raised it to his cracked lips for a taste. The luke-warm cream ale still possessed a discernable peppiness, apporting a not-unpleasant metallic tang with a hint of chicory, cumin and butter to the rear of his palette. He emptied the can, save the last sip which he sacrificed to the drain, topping the aluminum catcher with a column of ashes. He sucked hard on the red, inflating his lungs with smoke, and stood upright like a rotund tenor, allowing his diaphragm to fully expand. Feeling the pressure in his stomach, he simultaneously unstopped his throat and trachea expelling a thick ribbon of smoke, gas and air, opening the length of his esophagus and rattling his distended uvula with a deliciously dry throaty belch that rose in tandem with a grey cloud in a sonorous effluvium; a melange of the myriad tastes of the previous night: the bitter nut of the ale; a touch of tuna melt; Doritos; Slimjims; Twizzlers. His shoulders drooped forward over his gulched sternum and his head lolled back on his clavicles in a fleeting, sluttish buzz, akin to the remnants of a canister of Redi-Whip. An orange and black horseshoe floated across his hemeralopic spectrum and his back foot shifted, losing its bond with the beered linoleum. He stumbled back against the faded wood paneling before the door of his mobile home and slid to the floor.

A mild breeze swayed the waist-high weeds that had sprouted up on both sides of his hookup. He stuck out his head to reap its negligible effects, ruminating over the temptation to succumb to sleep for another hour—he didn't want to arrive at work later than usual. His head rolled back inside and he noticed another one of the signature red and white packages beneath his couch and bed, where Elvissa, a contemporary's porcine younger sister, continued to snore. She tended the checkout counter at the Speedi-Mart. How old was she, Jesse wondered. 18? 17? Old enough anyways, he reasoned, vaguely recalling her Schnapps-induced prelude to an ecdysiastic spectacle of which he was wholly uninterested and subsequently hurried her through himself after she lost consciousness.

He wasn't quite sure what exactly transpired, and he pondered the seminal competence of his chromosomal data—it had already proven steadfast, producing more than one set of familiar young eyes that bore into him from the sandbox with a divining intensity. He mouthed a quick prayer and consoled himself with the possibility that with Elvissa, penetration may have never technically been achieved. Elvissa choked for air and flopped onto her front, burying the sheet and offering up her large rump. Jesse eyed her hammy buttocks and generous thighs—still untouched by the saddle-bagging mulch of cellulite—but his head throbbed with the persistence of a bill collector.

He rose from the door, breathing in the miasmic sour stench of stale ale and smoke and B.O., as he stumbled over to retrieve the spent package beneath his couch and bed. He tore off the miles panel, opposite the Surgeon General's warning and subtracted five miles from his goal. Encouraged by the prospect of advancing a notch to his sheepskin Timber Mountain Pullover, he slipped into semiconsciousness; a deliciously mild reverie that lasted 30 or 40 seconds until a sharp flash of pain engulfed the corner of his mouth. He rose to his feet, gripping his lower back. Through the medicine cabinet mirror, he could see the empty aspirin bottle laughing and cursing him, as he examined the penultimate orange tooth that had been paining him since last November.

Side Two

A Day at the Races

MAB Tech zipped across the ticker at fifty-seven and one-eighth. Rumors of a hostile takeover by CyRed were spinning for a couple of weeks, and one of my Brothers at CyRed phoned me with news that the takeover was imminent. I purchased 50,000 shares at fifty-two and two-thirds at ten o'clock. With the price skyrocketing, obviously word was out on the street. And I was holding. Only one question remained: How much would CyRed pay for MAB?

My stomach still felt raw, as my trading limit was only a million and a half—if MAB Tech were to go south I could consider myself unemployed. But if it keeps up I'm going to be the big dick around here—something I've been planning for awhile now. I knew that if I didn't show some sack, I could expect to iron my own shirts and ride the PATH into my 30's.

Grace, the receptionist, approached my desk with a memo. She always delivered my messages personally, whereas the other secretaries e-mail them or drop them in my box.

Grace was a lot older—maybe thirty-five. She had put on about a dozen pounds in the last year, and all of her clothes looked about a size too small for her, but they were tight in all the right places. She smiled at me as she leaned over to place it on my desk and I could see her bra digging into her creamy flesh, the tight cups causing a smaller set of auxiliary breasts to heave over the top. She's like an out of work actress and she's got long blond hair and big painted lips and she's always saying things like, "You can just slide it in my box, if you'd like." And it kills me because I bet I could totally fuck her brains out if I wanted to. I mean, I definitely wanted to, but, dude, banging an older receptionist definitely undercuts your ambition; they'd never let me head the trading desk. Still, she totally has a lot of good fuck years left. Dude, she could walk into a bar and pick up any guy she wanted. But they'd be guys just like me—that is to say, guys just interested in casually fucking her until she started bugging them about a relationship. It's sad in a way, but that's the way things work. Getting seriously involved with Grace—even for a guy in his thirties—would be like finally pulling in big money and then buying a nice-looking Beamer with 70,000 miles on it.

Grace turned to walk out and I pushed my hand down on top of my erection. Dude, I'd fuck her like it was my job. But she probably wouldn't be very flattered in the morning upon being asked not to tell anyone. And women aren't capable of keeping secrets anyway. Then there's that golden rule about not dipping your pen in the company ink. Definitely good sense, I thought, lamenting that I couldn't have met Grace in a bar.

I glanced at my thirteen dollar Rolex. 12:45. My Brother said the hostile bid was to be formally announced at 2. I couldn't concentrate on any of my other work, not to mention that I kept picturing Grace leaning over my desk. So I decided to go to the park. I didn't have an abundance of time, but I had enough. I rose from my quadrant and grabbed the essentials out of my briefcase: five dollar Ray-Bans, faux silk handkerchief and the *Wall Street Journal.* Out on the street, standing in the gutter, it took over a minute to hail a cab.

"Bryant Park," I said, reaching up and handing the towelhead a ten. "As fast as you can."

"You got it," the towelhead said in surprisingly good English for a cabby as he lurched through the yellow light. He passed cars on the right and veered left around the stopped ones, just catching the yellow with each block on the timed lights. I reached down and tucked a corner of the handkerchief into the rim of my boxers, examining the passing women as we cruised uptown. There were quite a few professionally dressed minorities walking around—especially women. Affirmative action used to really piss me off. Back in high school, my first choice college rejected me while accepting this black kid in my class who didn't have anything near the grades and numbers I did. And the thing that really got me was that he was only like as black as Colin Powell, but just because he could truthfully check off that all-important box at the bottom of the application, he got in and I didn't. But now that I have a job, I could care less about affirmative action. I even kind of secretly support it. Because if they take a bunch of less qualified minorities and women—like they do at my company—then there's less competition. And even if they were as qualified as me, they'd only advance so far—all the top traders are white men. The towelhead jolted to a stop for a red light across from the Port Authority. He made it up to midtown in like four minutes. Some towelhead. But I anticipated the cross-town traffic, so I jumped out.

I crossed to the east side of 8th Ave and the regular group of Jesus freaks were screaming and yelling and singing and handing out flyers to the usual mix of crackheads, German tourists and transvestites. I waded through them, coming upon a dark-skinned black man at the end of the pack passing out flyers. He cast his glance exclusively at me and I wondered if I bore the look of someone desperate for spiritual guidance. I could barely discern his thick African accent as he chanted "My Lord, my Lord," cracking the flyers in his hand. But as I got closer, I realized he wasn't saying "My Lord, my Lord," but "Live show, live show." He was the first hawker in the line of adult stores, my suit giving me away as a hot prospect. I peered in the stores as I passed, all of the hawkers sensing my interest. The shelves were jammed with videos and gadgets and I couldn't believe how many guys with suits and briefcases were scanning the merchandise. I shook my head. What a bunch of losers.

It seemed like a fucking eternity, walking under the scaffolding of the Disney construction. I read the zipper as it posted the Dow until the pink-orange DON'T WALK sign stopped flashing, and I bolted across Broadway, catching sight of a few small white clumps change hands by the rack of pay phones in front of the Times Square subway entrance. I crossed 6th and then up the steps into the park. It's really incredible—when I was in high school, Bryant Park was a total crack den. Now it's like the hotspot of Manhattan. And with Disney's purchase of 42nd Street, I wondered what would happen to all the derelicts, whores and drug dealers. Where would they all go? Maybe, they'll just stay, I thought, picturing Minnie Mouse all strung out twirling a purse with Goofy standing next to her in a pink suit and a long feather in his hat.

The patched shadows of the leaves dotted the walkway of the park along 42nd Street and I strolled past the green benches, catching sight of a few chicks before turning right in front of the Bryant Park Cafe. Someone abandoned one of the coveted green chairs just as I passed in front of the steps of the library. I grabbed it and carried it over to the edge of the big lawn. I sat down and pushed my sunglasses up on the bridge of my nose before unfolding the Journal on my lap with the top half of the front page staring up at me.

This really hot Asian chick walked by with this bald white guy. She had nice legs and I took her in as I slid my hand through the slit in my right front pocket. After she passed, I picked out two women unfolding their lunches on the steps in front of the library. Nothing to write home about, but one sat with her knees apart and I caught a good view of the curve of her crotch, so I established her as my dead air safety. But the talent flowed steadily and a few times I actually made hard choices between the fleeting quality, rarely reverting to my safety on the steps. This hot fucking Indian chick in a silver lamé dress trotted by in high heels with four straps that shaped her chocolatey legs. Nice. With each step, there was a brief moment when the vent exposed an entire dark thigh. I took her in until she passed, and when I looked over towards 40th Street, I saw two Puerto Rican women approaching, but they were still too far off, so I caught the crotch on the steps until the Puerto Rican women got closer. Dude, they were *smokin*—definitely worth my time. A lot of times, Puerto Rican chicks can be fat ugly cows, but when they're good, they are the sexiest fucking women that exist. One of them showcased an unbelievable set of tits behind a beige body suit. The other one wore a miniskirt and black lace stockings and she had big pink lips and as they passed, I could hear them talking in Spanish. Bonus. The miniskirt cocked her ass back and forth, moving me onto the final stretch. Then I caught a lone black woman, wearing pants and walking with a hurried gait. She had a blue and white striped tubetop and her tits were bouncing all over the place. Anticipation is the key to success, I reminded myself, quickening, as I locked my arm in place, trying not to shake the Journal. I caught a glimpse of the blond crotch on the steps and she was looking right at me and I think she was on to me, but I couldn't worry about that because the black chick was getting closer. But my safety leaned over to gather up her garbage and I caught her tits in full view—always be prepared for the unexpected—and I hit the black woman as she passed in front of me and caught the side angle at the primo tit moment when she's just a few feet gone and then I shot back to my safety and unloaded just as she bobbed down for her Diet Coke.

Holy-fucking-shit. That was a good one. My shoulders dropped and the sun shone warmly on my face and I enjoyed a light buzz as I stretched out my pleasantly burning arm. When everything settled, I folded up the Journal and looked down. No seepage. I pulled away the handkerchief and balled it up, placing it in my good pocket. The blond chick on the steps was still looking right at me as her friend rambled on. She was totally on to me—maybe that's why it was so good. I wondered if maybe she might have even flashed me her cleavage on purpose. I lit a Benson and Hedges Light 100 and took a long first drag, letting out a stream of smoke as I stared right at her. But with our sunglasses neither one could really tell where the other was looking. Halfway through my cigarette, I discreetly dropped it on the lawn, out of view of the green-shirted groundskeepers, and stomped it out. I looked at my Rolex. 1:35. Plenty of time. I blew a kiss to my oh so luscious safety on the steps, but she didn't respond.

As the elevator rose above the teen floors, I heard people buzzing about MAB Tech. Dude, that's fucking *huge.* I stepped off the elevator and passed through the door. Grace sat at her desk and tossed her platinum blond mane, exposing neck at me. I hardly threw her a second look, hurrying over to my desk. MAB Tech was up to sixty-six and two-thirds. *Baby!* I sat back in my chair and watched it rise.

The Second Coming

I was standing up on the platform at the CASH ONLY line of the New Jersey Transit ticket window at the Port Authority, looking down the golden railing at a pudgy black woman begging for change. Her inside-out T-shirt stretched thin around her breasts, bearing a backwards distorted O.J. beneath the inverted caption: FREE AT LAST, FREE AT LAST, THANK GOD, I'M FREE AT LAST. A thin pink-orange sash covered her head and she looked about ten years younger than me—maybe 35—and from her timid style of begging, she appeared to have not been homeless very long. God, I didn't know what it was but she certainly inspired something in me. Even though I had masturbated earlier that morning—and one would think having just done it, one wouldn't have the urge—I still experienced a burning sensation and I felt the desire more than ever. As the saying goes: When it rains, it pours. I could feel the blood pulsing in the back of my neck with my vain attempt at fooling myself with yet another mental debate over my actions and desires, when I knew full well that in the end, I'll always succumb to my nature. I purchased my ticket for the racetrack and began down the golden railing towards the woman.

"Excuse me sir, I'm trying to get home to Atlanta. Can you spare some change?"

I could tell she hadn't fully developed her shtick as I dug into my pocket for a quarter. She stepped up to take it and I whispered to her, "I'll give you ten dollars if you let me feel your breasts."

She didn't look surprised or scared, but nodded hesitantly as though trying to figure a catch. I bet I could have gotten her for five—my allocation was recently cut back and I had to be careful with my money.

She walked alongside me, one pace behind. I was walking fast although I had no idea where to go. The restroom seemed the only sanctuary one would ever find in the Port Authority, so we took the escalator down to the level below ground. We turned the corner and when I saw that no one was near the men's room, I hurried her inside. I went to the last stall, but the door was stuck so we went into the next one and I latched the full-length metal door. Then I heard groans from the next stall, realizing two other people were using the bathroom for a physical transaction. This didn't seem to faze her and she yanked the hem of her T-shirt from under her cracked leather belt.

"No," I said, "please leave them covered." I approached her and could see she wasn't wearing a bra. Although they sagged a bit, they still possessed a supple consistency, pendulous and plentiful. Her large nipples grew hard as stones and I was straining against my zipper as I groped her through her T-shirt.

"Be not afraid," I said undoing my zipper. Her face flickered with the slightest recognition that seemed to say:

Here's the catch—there always is one. I began humping her soft belly through her T-shirt. She put on an indifferent expression, staring sideways as I resumed fondling her breasts. Upon closing my eyes, I saw myself as a boy—strange as my first experience with a woman occurred when I was 33—and I was running barefoot through the pasture towards our house and the sun felt warm on my back and I could smell the peach pie my mother had set on the sill and I cupped her flesh and pushed upward and came wonderfully, completely, even though it burned some and when I opened my eyes, she was staring down at the opaque blob covering O.J. Simpson's backward stretched visage.

"Oh, God, I'm sorry," I said, tearing off a strip of toilet paper to wipe off her shirt. She looked at me and grabbed the toilet paper, blindly padding her shirt, while staring at me with raised eyebrows. I pulled the ten out of my pocket and handed it to her. Then I dug back in and extracted another two dollars.

"I'm sorry about your shirt," I said.

She took the money and didn't say anything. When I looked down, I noticed a grey bead that had fallen on her shoe and I tore off another strip of toilet paper and bent down to clean it up. My knees audibly cracked.

"Oh, God, Oh God, it hurts!" a broken young male voice groaned from the next stall. I could smell smoke and sulfur and my mouth went dry. My knees cracked again as I rose and hurried her out of the stall.

"Are you hungry?" I asked her.

She shrugged.

"I'm going to buy a cup of coffee," I said, escorting her from the bathroom. "Could I buy you something to eat?"

She nodded and followed me out. The young male voice in the next stall resonated in my ear as we approached Au Bon Pain. I ordered a regular coffee and a peach danish.

"Anything else?" the young black attendant asked me, casting her wary glance at the woman.

I nodded over to her.

"A plain bagel," she said.

"Butter or cream cheese."

"Plain," she repeated.

She handed over the food and I passed a five over the counter. Watching the bill disappear in the register, I felt guilty for having considered offering the woman a mere five dollars. The attendant handed me the change and without looking I gave it to the woman.

"God Bless You," she said and walked away.

Although I felt rather edgy about what I'd done, I couldn't help closing my eyes on the bus to indulge in the recollection of the scene. The guilt subsided and I felt light and optimistic about the track. But I knew the image of this woman saying "God Bless You," would remain etched in my mind—how ironic.

When I opened my eyes, Giants Stadium and Byrne Arena rose high above the swamp. The racetrack looked like a giant glass pyramid that had been toppled over. I faced forward and pondered whether or not my actions merited confession; I didn't fornicate. And I didn't hurt her. It wasn't so different from when I masturbated earlier that morning—and I certainly wasn't in the habit of confessing each time I did that.

Clutching my tickets and staring up at the overcast sky, I still felt a measure of guilt. I confessed my actions to God; an act I reserved for such complex situations. The sun spilled through a gap in the clouds, and I felt the guilt subsiding after hitting a longshot in the first race. Suddenly, a hand crashed down on my shoulder. My heart lurched.

"Hey! Father Izzy!"

Oh God, one of my parishioners! I slowly turned, my eyes following the wrist up to the elbow to the crooked smile of Joey Fratella. I let out a sigh of relief. Although it was strange to see him at the racetrack, as he was a boy of twelve when I came to St. Jude's in Lodensack twelve years ago. But then I realized it was probably equally disconcerting for him to see an ordained priest holding tickets. He reached out and shook my hand.

"Hello, Giuseppe," I said.

"Hiya, Father. You know, aside from my mom, you're the only one who still calls me that?" He laughed. "Fancy seeing you here. I mean—not that there's anything wrong with that—I just never imagined, you know, you don't think about running into a priest at the racetrack. But what the heck. They gotta let you break free once in a while, don't they? You're only human like the rest of us."

"Yes. Only human," I parroted back to him, managing a nod.

"After all, the Pope was at Aqueduct just last week."

"Yes," I laughed. "Yes, that's right."

He sat down next to me and my stomach began to settle.

"Who do you have for the next race, Father?"

"I've got Stone's Throw to place," I said.

"So do I!" Giuseppe exclaimed, his face lighting up as though holding the same ticket as a priest guaranteed a win.

"Listen, Father, do you think maybe you could say a Hail Mary or something for the next race?"

I laughed until I realized he was perfectly serious.

"Sure," I said. "Why don't we say one together."

Giuseppe looked over his shoulder and then back at me.

"You mean out loud?"

"I suppose you can say it to yourself," I said.

"Okay. Tell me when so that we can both start at the same time."

"Okay," I said.

"Oh and do you think maybe you could add just a little something extra, Father? For the horse."

"Sure," I said.

He closed his eyes and we both prayed. Stone's Throw placed paying $8.60. I fared well the rest of the day. And even after subtracting the money I gave to the woman, I came out on top $40.

Let Them Have New Jersey

If you do the job on her from behind," George said, "it increases the odds that you'll get a boy."

"*Bull*shit," I said.

"And if it happens when your wife's on top you're more likely to get a girl," he said, stepping over the threshold into the breakroom. John the biker was sitting with Sal and I knew Georgie was avoiding John, so I plopped down at the table in the corner so's to make it my choice where we sat.

"I got the new pictures back," John said.

"Let's see em," Sal said.

John handed Sal some glossies of his son.

"Christ," Sal said. "He's huge."

"He's starting Kindergarten a year early," John said. "We had him take the test and he scored real high. We just made the cutoff, so-"

"-Is he gonna go to St. Jude's?" Sal asked.

"Hell no," John said.

"What district are you in? River?"

"Yeah."

"Isn't River starting to go black?"

"They got a couple of em over there, but it's not as bad as everyone says." John adjusted the tomato-red pipe wrench hanging down to his knee. "He'll know how to defend himself."

"They got a few Portereekins, too," Sal said.

John shrugged, annoyed.

"Suppose you had a button," Sal said, "that could wipe out an entire race. Which one would you choose?"

John rolled his eyes.

"Well, okay," Sal said. "But who would be your second choice?"

"The fucking Jews."

"The *Jooz*?"

"Definitely."

"You would get ridda the Jooz before the Portereekins?"

John nodded.

"Before all the sand nigguhs?"

"You're going to need to fill up your tank sooner or later," John deadpanned.

"That's true." Sal laughed. He crumpled an empty pack of Merits and cocked his head and squinted at John. "*Before the Portereekins*?"

"Who told you this?" I asked George.

"I read it in the Home Medical Journal."

"What's that?"

"It's a book."

"Oh."

Georgie lit up a Newport. He had been smoking them for a couple of weeks which was strange because Marlboro was his brand since we were kids.

"See, male sperms are shaped like a Y," Georgie said, demonstrating with his hands, "and female sperms are like an X."

"All niggers should swim back to Africa and they should pack a homo under each arm," John said. "Africa this, Africa that. If it's such a great place, why don't they go the fuck back?"

"What about that guy who wants us to give em three states so all the blacks can live there by themselves?"

"Where do I sign?" John folded his arms.

"You'd give it to em?" Sal said.

"I'd give them Montana, Idaho and North Dakota right now."

"Yeah? Suppose they wanted Jersey."

"If all of them would come here and we built a concrete wall around the state so I'd never have to lay eyes on another fucking nigger again? I'd let them have New Jersey."

"I'll show it to you next time you're over," George said. "See, the female sperms are better swimmers because the X-shape gives them an extra leg kicking. So if your wife's on top, you're more likely to get a girl. But from behind, it sends them right to the womb and the male sperms have a better shot."

"Really?"

"Sure. I'm not talkin definite. The odds are just cocked a little in your favor. You know, maybe 60-40."

"I would send them gas money," John said. "Somebody's gotta do it. You think those people in Idaho would be any happier?" John tugged at the material of his black T-shirt—one of many that bore flames and white hoods. Before him, I didn't even know they had the KKK in New Jersey.

"Shit," I said. "You got two boys, too."

George smiled. "How long have you been trying for?"

I leaned in close to him. I could smell the stale menthol mixing with the Brut on his chin. "A year and a half."

"How often are you doing the job on her?"

"Almost every night. And sometimes she gets me in the morning, before I run off to the shower. It's fucked up. I mean

I'm bangin the crap outta her and its not even fun anymore. It's time to make love she says, but-" I dropped to a whisper, "there's no love there. It's just fucking, you know, like a machine and it's become more of a chore than anything."

"Makin' love," George hissed. "You know what making love is?"

I shook my head.

"That's what my wife's doin when I'm FUCKIN THE SHIT OUTTA HER!"

I didn't laugh.

"So what's your deal?" George cracked a thin smile. "Are you shooting blanks?"

"I don't know." I peeled the label off my bottle.

"Have you gotten tested?"

"My wife went to the doctor. He said she's OK."

"What about you?"

"Fuck that. I aint jacking off into a test tube."

"Aww get over it. Doctors can do things."

"What things?"

"You know...things." George leaned in close and whispered: "I had a little help with Robby."

"You mean like...artificial stamination?"

"It's not that big of a deal. The nurse set me up in a room with a couple of skin mags and I shot a load in a cup and they took like this little turkey baster and sucked it up and shot it into my wife."

"Really?"

"Yeahhhhh," he hissed.

"Fuck that. It aint natchrul."

"It's perfectly natural. It's not like they used somebody else's."

"I don't know. Sometimes I'm not even sure I want kids." I flung my bottle across the room smashing it in the corner just above the garbage can. John the biker looked up. My little trick hadn't been working lately; hardly any of the pieces of glass fell into the can.

"What do you mean you don't want kids?" George said.

"Look at the news. The world's becoming more and more of a shithole by the day. Why would I want to bring anybody else into it?"

I thought about Richie, this old guy who had worked at the Water Company since after The War. He was in some kind of death squad or something in Japan and I guess it fucked him up some. But once he told me that it wasn't The War that fucked him up, but the studying he did after his tour. He got to go to some fancy school in England on the G.I. Bill. The Sore-done or something. And I guess he started to learn about some of the shit he was doing over there. Anyways, his nickname at the W-C was Doom, because he was always talking about how the world was coming to an end.

"Ya better getcher kicks before the whole shithouse goes up in flames," he used to say to me, under his breath. They all thought he was off his chair. I mean he *was* definitely nuts, but sometimes some of the shit he used to go on about really made sense. He finally retired last year, after fifty years at the Water Company.

"You know who you're starting to sound like," Georgie said, "Dooooooom!" His eyes got all big and he waved his hands.

"Fuck you," I said.

George laughed. "You *have* to have kids!" he said, smiling like it was a big joke or something.

"Who says?"

"Nobody *says* but, you know, everybody has kids. Whether or not the world explodes don't make a lick of difference. Not only that, you're the only son. You have to carry on your family name. Hasn't your father explained that to you by now?"

"No," I said. "My father, you know, he don't talk too much anymore."

"Oh, right," George said.

I thought about the made-for-TV movie I watched the night before about a guy and his wife and their daughter who got run over by a drunk driver. The guy who killed her got out of jail after only a couple of years and they led this big court battle to make tougher punishments for drunk drivers and the thing happily ended with the woman discovering she was pregnant. I turned it off as soon as it was over because people in real life don't pick up the pieces like that. After my brother was killed, my parents weren't interested in leading some kind of crusade against drunk drivers. I mean, my brother was *dead*. And the guy who crashed into him was killed, too. His life was taken for taking my brother, so, you know, justice was served. But my father, he really wanted to see my brother play pro ball. Since he was killed, well my father just kind of talks about the weather. Sometimes he says things like if my brother were still alive. And my mother is just kind of quiet and nervous, so you know, they never really said anything to me when my wife didn't get pregnant right away. Not like Georgie's parents, who while he was still just engaged, were saying things out loud at barbecues about how he and his wife better get cracking right away. I just don't know. And, honestly, I don't know how Georgie affords his boys on his salary.

"You want your boys to go to college?" I asked George, rising to pick up the broken glass.

"You're goddamn right they're going to college. And not to some community college for a junior degree, neither. They're gonna go to a real four-year university."

"Aren't you worried about how much it's going to cost once Nicky graduates high school?" I swept up the shards with the butt of my hand.

"I know how much it's going to cost."

"Really?"

"A hundred and fifty-eight thousand dollars." George adjusted his belt. "I figured it out on my calculator. You gotta get em scholarships. It's the only way."

"That's easy for you. You got boys. Suppose I end up with a girl."

"They got scholarships for them too."

"They do?"

"Sure."

"I don't know."

"I don't know why you hate the Jooz so much," Sal said. "First off, they're white-"

"They're *not* white," John the biker interrupted. "They've got nigger hair."

"Oh for Chrissakes, John, they're white enough. A lot of Italians got brillo for hair too, so I hope you're not planning on bumping us off next. Second of all the Jooz don't cause any trouble. I'd definitely zap the Portereekins second. All that loud fuckin music they play while layin their greasy car parts all over the place and yappin in Spanish? No question. Hell, at least the Jooz speak English."

"There are few things I hate more than a dirty fucking Jew." John unfolded his thick arms and massaged his faded tattoos before standing. The large key ring hanging from his belt jangled as he walked past me and I caught a glimpse of a gold circular tag with three K's cut out of it over the words IN GOOD STANDING.

"I'm getting pretty tired of John and all his notsee bullshit," George said.

"He gets a little crazy about that stuff," I said.

"I mean he's fucked up. Right or wrong?" George looked a little huffed up.

"Right," I said.

"Christ," George said. "I'd need *ten* buttons before I got around to zapping the Jews."

"Yeah." I cleaned up the rest of my trash and stepped in the toilet. As I sat down on the can, I could hear the quick trot of the lab supervisor getting louder in the hall and stopping in the breakroom.

"Hi, John," she said.

"I've got new pictures of Patrick," John said.

"Oh, Jesus, John!"

"What?"

"That is the most offensive thing I have ever, ever seen," she said in a grave voice.

"I am a member."

"I don't care. That is completely inappropriate. If I see you wearing that again in the lab, I'm going to speak to Darrel."

"Go ahead. And I'll get the A.C.L.U. down here for infringing my right to free speech."

"Oh, John! Honestly!"

"What?! You got these summer helps from Harriston running around here in their X hats and that's okay; but then I'm not allowed to wear a shirt bearing a separatist organization of which I am a member?"

"I don't know. It just...offends me. And the other summer helps will see it."

"Whatever. I mean I know I'm not a role model, but just because I'm a racist doesn't mean I'm a bad person."

She let out a long sigh. "Let's see."

"Here. You can take one of the little ones."

"He's really big," she said.

"He'll be starting Kindergarten next year," John said.

"Is he going to go to St.-"

I drowned out the rest of their conversation with a double flush.

Junior High School Bitches

They had gone into extra innings.

Jack McDowell was pitching and Edgar Martinez doubled, sending Junior home for the winning run. The Yankees lost game five against Seattle and their much anticipated 1995 post-strike season was over. Dominic propped himself up on an elbow and hocked up a loogie, surveying the debris that covered his coffee table. He selected an empty pint container of Cherry Garcia and the cut tip of a Phillies cigar along with its guts spilled across the vacant spot. Dominic dropped the loogie into the container and wung it neatly to the top of his overflowing garbage can.

"I can't believe they fuckin blew it," Dominic said, snatching the remote control. He aimed it at his TV which was propped up on the right side with a stack of law books, opposite a cinder block on the left. He lit a Marlboro Light and took the blunt from Ernie and sat back in his spot on the couch, alternating between the Marlboro and the blunt. After a few hits, he passed the blunt to me. I'm not much of a pot smoker, but I drew a hit. It went down smoothly and I took another pull of the sweet-tasting blunt. Dominic coughed up another thick frog, and not finding a convenient place of deposit, swallowed it.

After flunking the bar a second time, Dominic pointedly decided to give himself enough time before a third go, "I'm not going to become more of a fuckup than JFK Jr.," was how he put it. I don't know why Dominic ever went to law school; his father was the long-standing mayor of Lodensack, NJ, his home town, and I suppose that was as good a reason as any. I didn't ask him much about it, as it was obviously a touchy subject. After flunking the second time, he found a full time job in a bar. He grew out his hair and pierced his eyebrow and started making good money in tips. The modest amount of discipline he still possessed was expended in working up a set of "beach muscles," as he called them. He began acquiring more phone numbers, and with the lengthening of his hair and his triceps bulging like snakes around his arms, the tip money got better and so did the phone numbers. A political scion himself, he partied like a Kennedy, not waking until 3 or 4 in the afternoon to shower for work. As he grew more settled in the bar, I doubted he would ever take the bar exam again, thinking what a damn shame, all that money and work expended on years of college and law school wasted; but a nagging feeling came over me as I remembered that after four years, I remained a copy editor who still couldn't afford to live in Manhattan. And I still hadn't put any of my own stuff down on paper, nor did I feel terribly inspired to do so. And while the sheer number of lawyers in the world ensured a dog-eat-dog profession, the odds were still worse if you wanted to become a writer. And here I was at age 26, having still not surpassed the mental fits and starts of Page One. I began to feel the self-conscious twitch of marijuana engulf my upper body.

"Das some fucked up *shit*, yo!" Ernie exclaimed, rising from the table and grabbing the smoldering blunt from my docile hand. "Motherfuckers ahead two games to zero. Three games left in Seattle and they drop all motherfucking three." Ernie locked his lips around the fat joint.

"They would have lost to Cleveland anyway, yo." Albert sat back in his beanbag, palming his belly crunched between his lap and his chest like a crystal ball.

I had a few beers before stopping over, but they were wearing off and the marijuana was making me fidget. I don't know why I smoked to begin with—the last time was probably when Dominic and I were in the dorm at Gample. I was more of a drinker. I don't consider myself an alcoholic, but during the last year and a half, I had been drinking quite a bit. I don't remember if my depression stemmed from my inability to write, or vice-versa. It was all one cold grey soup, and alcohol disentangled these two conditions so that I could deal with them separately. Unfortunately, I never really felt good, and most of what I managed to scribble never amounted to anything worth developing.

It was an especially cloudy day. One in which a nagging urgency branched out from my gut through my entire body, halting concentration to the point that I couldn't connect words in a book, or even follow the TV. After returning from the office, I had begun "running laps" as I referred to it when I would pace from the bathroom, to sitting on my couch, to lying on my bed before jetting back to the bathroom for another inspection. It's good to get out when this happens, so I went to a bar to kill time before arriving at Dominic's. And I guess my acceptance of the blunt was akin to the strategy of a trailing basketball team committing a foul with only seconds left; a last ditch effort to regain possession for a prayer shot.

But their weed was strong and I felt as though I was losing control of my facial expressions. I itched for a drink and had lost patience waiting for Dominic to offer me one. The bugs had begun crawling up the back of my neck.

"You got any beers?" I hurriedly asked. Talking seemed an incredible chore.

"Hey Bert and Ernie," Dominic asked, his eyes still trained on the glow of the TV, "do we got any beers?"

Albert shook his head with remorse, as though hearing about a pregnant woman taking a stray bullet.

"We gah some Cisco," Ernie piped up.

"I need beer," I said, looking to counter the bugs.

"Okay," Dominic pointed blindly, "don't go to the store downstairs. Fuckin rip-off. Turn right and then right at the corner and there's a deli right there and they got 40's real cheap. It's like three bucks for Budweiser."

"Two-eighty-six after tax, bro," Albert proclaimed.

I didn't bother asking if anyone wanted to step out with me. The air felt cool and good and after the haze of Dominic's apartment, the rooftops took on a heightened clarity against the black sky. Even though we had both been working in Manhattan for a few years, I hadn't seen much of Dominic since we graduated from Gample. I really couldn't believe he was living with two Latinos, as I remembered some remark he made a few years ago about the abundance of Puerto Ricans in the neighborhood I grew up in. But it was a nice big apartment they shared in Gramercy. Ernie landed Dominic his job in the bar and Albert worked at the video store across the street. "They're good guys—very responsible," Dominic had earlier proclaimed on the phone. I found the Bud 40's on the bottom shelf of the cooler and carried one up to the counter and the guy rang it up. Two-eighty-six.

I felt claustrophobic and mildly paranoid under the harsh lighting of the deli and I asked the attendant to ring up a second bottle. I paid and stuffed my change into my pocket without counting it and pulled open the door. I cradled the bag of 40's like an unruly child as I stepped back to Dominic's place and began on the stairs.

"No fuckin way, yo!" Ernie professed, as I stepped inside, smacking the back of his fingers against the palm of his other hand.

"Oh, she totally will," Dominic said. "She's going to be like Keith Richards. She'll have a coma every couple of years but she'll live to be an old lady."

"Yo check it out!" Ernie turned towards me. "This motherfucker think Courtney Love gonna live past the 20th Century."

"I really don't think," I said, feeling the cold heft of the 40's in my arm, "that she's going to see the light of 1998."

"Yeah, *right*?"

I left the 40 in its paper sheath and drained half the bottle, the liquid settling like a cool fist in my gut.

"She make it," Albert said, drawing a pull off a fresh blunt. "Just because. Check it out; suicide gonna go *down* in 1999, yo. People want to *see* the 21st century. Who the fuck kill theyself in 1999? You crazy, yo. Because everyone think as soon as it become 2000, cars gonna fly, or we all have a watch on our wrist like motherfuckin Dick Tracy. But then after it happen and everyone see its like the same fucked up shit? Gonna be a motherfuckin *let*down. People gonna drop like *flies* after tha shit blows over, yo. Thas why I put mah money on the year 2*000*."

"Ahhight check it out, yo. Dominic think she gonna be a oh lady. Albert think she gonna die between two thousand and two thousand and one. I *know* she not gonna be around for that party, yo. I betchou fifty dolluhs each."

"So," Dominic sat up, "if she lives to the year 2001, you and Albert pay me fifty bucks each?"

"Yeah," Ernie nodded with conviction.

"And then if she dies during the year 2000, we pay

Albert?"

"Yeah, thas right. And if she die in the nineties? Motherfuckers gonna be payin me some *money*!"

"I'm in," Dominic said. I found it odd that Dominic unflinchingly made a bet that he hoped wouldn't be reconciled for another six years.

"Bet," Albert said. He had smoked the Philly down to its last third. "You want this?" He looked at me. I shook my head. My face was still crawling.

"Ernie," Albert said.

"Throw it, yo."

Albert went deep, spiraling the thick joint in a long arc over the coffee table and across the room. Ernie caught it in his cupped fingers, but burned himself as he tried to grab it. "*Got*damn!" The blunt fell to the floor and he scooped it up, licked his fingertip and pressed out the smoldering cinder that had dropped on the carpet. Similar burn marks surrounded Ernie's butterfly chair like automatic gunfire.

"Her little girl gonna be in Playboy," Albert said, palming his belly.

"*Who*?" Ernie asked.

"Courtney Love little girl."

"Maybe," Ernie said.

Dominic began surfing the channels, informing me that they had a scrambler which provided them with every channel on cable including the Pay-Per-Views, free of charge. He stopped for the skin segment in the opening teaser for *Hard Copy*.

"Leave that, yo!" Ernie pointed at the oiled row of bikini-clad breasts bouncing in harmony.

"Fuck that," Dominic said, "they show you the whole thing in the opening credits. That's all the tits you gonna see, bro."

I found it odd how they drooled over the opening credits of *Inside Edition* like a couple of cartoon icons while a string of porn ads was playing on public access channel 35—not to mention their scrambler, which provided them with soft porn on Playboy and Spice. Dominic flipped to *A Current Affair* which displayed some models in thong bikinis, their bare breasts veiled under a scrambled patch.

"See? They replay the same shit at the end. The rest is bullshit." Dominic flipped to another tabloid show. They still headlined with stories on the aftermath of The Trial. *Entertainment Tonight* played a promo regarding his visiting rights with his children, flashing a photo of the two catalogish mulatto youngsters, and then I realized it wasn't *E.T.*, but a show hosted by Connie Chung.

"Thas gonna be some *fucked* up chiljren, yo," Ernie said.

"They gonna be like the *Ken*nedys," Albert said sitting up from his beanbag as though 3G's worked against his head. "The media gonna follow they asses all through *ev*ry damn thing. When they start getting fucked up and arrested and datin people in Hollywood an shit? Iss gonna be in *all* the magazines, yo." He settled back in his beanbag. "Who wanna bet O.J. daughter be in Playboy?"

No one took him up.

"When you gonna be a lawyer Dominic?" Ernie said, eyeing the Dream Team.

I sat forward.

"Eventually," Dominic said.

"Johnnie Cochran be getting some *pussy*, yo." Ernie looked over to Albert to back him up. Albert scrunched his mouth to one side and nodded yes in slo-mo.

Dominic shrugged. Back in the dorm at Gample, he played sloppy seconds to Tom Cruise like most clean-cut white boys in college during the late 80's. But Dominic worked it better than the rest of us. I figured he had gotten it from the Mayor, as I had heard stories about Dominic Sr. from a guy at Gample who was from Lodensack. He informed me that the

Mayor had payrolled numerous secretaries who weren't exactly selected for their typing skills. And not only did Dominic Sr. not conceal these arrangements, he flaunted them. Apparently, the Mayor preferred single mothers, as their dependence on a steady paycheck helped keep the greater lid on his dalliance. I met him once at Dominic's house, standing in front of their fireplace and shaking hands with the Mayor in front of a picture of him with the Pope. A short, stocky, comb-over, the Mayor looked like a stereotypical local Democratic politician from New Jersey. And I wondered why—in this age of scandal—the local newspaper respected his philandering, but the guy from Lodensack told me that the journalists didn't so much respect Dominic's dad as fear him. The guy claimed that someone penned a story about a kickback scheme involving loans for small businesses, but the managing editor of the paper killed it. The following day, the journalist was unceremoniously pulled over by a policeman who discovered a sizable bag of coke under his seat. I asked him how he knew all of this and he responded that the journalist was his father.

I wondered what the mayor was like as a young man. And as I further considered Dominic Jr.'s impressive career as a womanizer—one that unlike his father's, didn't require a carrot or a stick—I wondered if Dominic wasn't merely embarked on some kind of top-secret training to one day join the ranks of the Democratic Party.

Dominic lit up a Marlboro light.

"Since when do you smoke cigarettes?" I asked him. When we were at Gample, he played attack on the lacrosse team.

"You know, in the bar and all."

"Dominic be smoking a *lot*," Ernie said, wrapping his lips around a fresh blunt. I was still feeling the effects of my three pulls and these two guys just kept puffing away. I couldn't believe they were still coherent, let alone carrying on a conversation. But then I raised my 40 and remembered that I drank an awful lot of beer.

"Look at this motherfucker," Dominic turned to me, "with a goddamn Phillies blunt in his mouth telling me I smoke too much."

"Smoke to get high, not to die, yo," Ernie said.

"The Marlboro Man be dead," Albert proclaimed.

"That's bullshit," Dominic said.

"*Fuck* you. I read his o*bit*uary. In the motherfuckin New York *Times*."

"You fulla shit, Albert," Ernie said. "You don't read but People Magazine."

"I was on the *sub*way, bitch. Somebody else reading the paper while I checkin out the back *page*. Motherfucker's dead as Elvis, yo. 73 years ole. He died uh lung cancer."

"The Marlboro Man died uh lung cancer?" Ernie asked.

"Thas fuckin re*dem*ption, yo." Albert said.

"What the fuck are you talking about?" Dominic said, hocking up another loogie. "He was 73. That's a year longer than he was supposed to live."

The phone rang. Dominic picked up. He mouthed 'Paul' over to Ernie.

"Tell that motherfucker I said *Hakuna-matata*."

"Paul says your boy never showed up."

"Wha time he sposed to be there?"

"You talk to him." Dominic tossed him the receiver but the cord took hold just before Ernie could grab it and the receiver recoiled with a thud onto the carpet.

"Shit..." Ernie stood and retrieved the phone.

"*Hakuna-matata,* motherfucker....huh?...that mean chill duh fuck out, yo....what time he spose be there?...No I said, e*lev*en, yo...Den you *heard* me wrong." Ernie checked his wrist but he didn't have a watch. He glanced at the TV as Dominic flipped by the closing credits of *Chicago Hope*. "Iss not even eleven now..." The receiver dropped under his chin. "Motherfucker put me on hold, yo, *damn*!...He there? See I *tole* you, eleven o'clock, yo...yeah," Ernie laughed and shook his head. "*Hakuna-matata,* motherfucker!" He replaced the receiver and crashed back down in his chair. The phone rang again.

"Gah-*damn*," Ernie said.

Dominic picked it up, his face going slack as he let out a tired hello. "Hi, Grace.......I don't think so.......I'm really busy.......Wait, hold on." Dominic looked over at me. "My friend here isn't busy."

My eyes popped. I shook my head no. Dominic looked at me like I had no idea.

"Yes. He's very nice. Much nicer than me.......Yes I'll give it to him. Okay. Bye, Grace."

"What the fuck are you doing?" I asked him.

"That's a good-looking woman," Dominic said, scribbling down her address.

"She gah some big-ass titties, yo," Ernie added.

I looked over to Albert for verification and he slowly shook his head yes.

"Then how come you don't fuck her?"

"Dude, I'm *beat*."

Dominic fucked girls with the ease and decisiveness with which I stepped outside to buy my beer; the thought of going with one of his discards turned my stomach.

"She's like an actor, only she's still a receptionist. She's 35 and a platinum blond and she puts back young dick. Just tell her how beautiful you think she is and that you can't believe that they keep letting Sharon Stone make shitty movies while she answers phones." Dominic tossed me her phone number.

I stuffed it into my pocket without looking.

"Yo, I'll fuck her," Ernie sat up.

"Yeah, right," Dominic said.

I broke the cap on my second 40. Sure. I'll call her. She'll become an actress. Dominic will become a lawyer. I'll become a writer. Courtney Love will become a grandmother and *next* year, Yanks will go all the way.

"You know what's fucked up?" Dominic sat up and began zapping the channels. "My wife is somewhere in junior high school now."

"You wife aint even motherfuckin *born* yet," Ernie said. Albert backed him up with a laugh.

"I'll probably get married in eight years when I'm 34, to a 22 year old after she graduates college. That means she's 14 right now. That's junior high."

"That mean she startin to get *fucked* right now!" Ernie laughed.

"Ho, shit!" Albert said.

"Not my wife," Dominic said.

"How come you want to marry a girl?" Ernie asked.

"'Cause I want huh ass still lookin good when I be olduh, yo," Dominic said, imitating Ernie.

"Thas why we got di*vor*ce," Ernie said "You marry who you wanna fuck *now*. And when she start to get all wrinkled up and saggy, you outta there like Mandela. *Then* you marry your little junior high school bitch and ten years later you dump *her* saggin ass and find yourself a secretary or a manicurist half your age plus *five*, yo, and then you settle down for good. She still be lookin young and her pussy still be tight until you don't give a fuck no more and then you got a bitch nurse your ass til *death*, yo."

"I hear that." Albert palmed his belly.

"Fuck that," Dominic said. "I'm gonna do it right the first time." He surfed three more channels before tossing the remote control to Ernie. I wondered what Dominic knew or thought about his father.

"Gah*damn*!" Ernie smacked his hand on one of the coffee tables. "I still can't believe dem mothuhfuckin Yankees. *Shit.*"

"What are you gonna do?" I said, just to say something to regain control of my tongue. I was starting to feel like myself again. "I'm beat," I said, draining the 40 as I rose. The bugs were almost gone.

"Alright, brother." Dominic got up on an elbow. "If you ever don't feel like taking the PATH back home, you can crash here." He gestured at the continuous line of couch.

"Thanks," I said, clasping his hand. I shook hands with Ernie and Albert.

"Yeah stop by any time, yo," Ernie said. "We always here."

Albert slowly nodded.

I closed the door and stepped outside, footing it towards 23rd Street, feeling my pockets for a dollar bill. I watched a man in a suit stagger out of a taxi and fish his keys out of the gutter. Suddenly I could see Dominic as a successful lawyer with his junior high school wife and his own TV commercials. I could even see him on the campaign trail, replacing his father as mayor. Meanwhile I was but a mediocre copy editor in a mid-sized publishing house—a job I had been gridlocked in for almost four years. Dominic was set up in a nice pad in Gramercy pulling in seven bills a week, living the life every guy dreams of—I could hardly say the same about myself, and I felt like a shithead for judging him.

Traffic weaved around a crouched bus and I passed a Barnes & Noble with twenty copies of Newt's novel propped up in the window, the Speaker's fat face and helmet hairdo dominating the display. In the light, I dug out Grace's address and number. It was five blocks away. A payphone stood on the corner and I returned the dollar to my pocket and extracted a quarter and punched in Grace's number. My throat went dry.

"Hello?" a dreamy voice answered.

"Uhh, hi, I'm Dominic's friend."

"You have a nice voice," she said.

"So do you," I replied, feeling my shoulders relax.

"You're not mentally unstable, are you?"

"Yes."

"Then come over." She hung up the phone without saying good-bye. Just like in the movies.

Seven minutes later, I caught my breath in front of her door and pressed the button.

"Just a minute!" she called through the door.

I stood there for literally a minute before she slid back the cover of the eyepiece. I heard the chain and then the clanking twist of the deadbolt. The door opened and she greeted me. Her face was freshly made up and she wore cotton slippers and a white T-shirt tucked into worn blue jeans. And Ernie was right; she did have some big-ass titties. For a split second I felt crass and flashed on inviting her to get a cup of coffee or some kind of Holden Caulfield move.

"Hi," I managed.

"Please come in," she said, taking my hand, which I thought an odd gesture. She led me to her kitchen and offered me a cup of tea.

"Yes, please," I said, eyeing the generous curve of her shirt. The clouds have a way of curtailing your sexual appetite; a cruel and unambiguous jab to remind you—mentally and physically—that things are not as they should be. So it encouraged me to feel my blood circulating, to feel a break in the stagnation. Grace sat in front of a small bookshelf that contained Greek Dramas, Shakespeare, Beckett, Brecht, Tennessee Williams and Arthur Miller. She swiftly led us through the preliminary bullshit, but as it is bullshit, I didn't mind. We soon arrived at an actual conversation, laced with opinions, observations and rebuttals. She communicated with poise and wit and I don't think I could possibly explain what a pleasure it was at that moment just to converse with an attractive, educated woman—not to mention having felt desire for the first time in weeks. After my second cup of tea, I began to worry that I might be in for some of that Holden Caulfield bullshit after all.

We talked through another cup and she asked me about my job at the publishing house.

"Well," she said, "I'm sure you're making connections that will help you get published."

I nodded, charmed by her assumption that anyone working in a publishing house was an aspiring writer. I asked her about acting and she talked a blue streak about some upcoming auditions and gay directors and how she hated L.A. and the snail-like progression of a day on a movie set. My eyes dropped to her chafed hands and when she smiled, a tiny network of wrinkles branched out from her eyes. But she projected a radiant energy far more exuberant than anything I possessed and when we started talking about Baudelaire, I wondered why she would ever call Dominic. Maybe with a young man she could still dream and I realized that at least with Dominic there wouldn't be any bullshit. I gazed into her eyes, grey with chips of blue and green and hazel and she stared back with the focused intensity of a newscaster. I couldn't break from the lock of her glance. Pure Hollywood.

"I don't know much about the entertainment industry," I said, "but it truly baffles me that Hollywood signs people like

Sharon Stone to make one crappy movie after another, while they keep you hidden away out here answering phones." The words flew out of my mouth and I regretted using Sharon Stone.

"You're very sweet." She stood and took my hand again and I rose. She clasped her hands around my neck and I stared into her eyes, multi-colored like a painter's palette. She kissed me patiently on the lips and pulled away. I drew her in again and kissed her and she moaned softly, just like in the movies. She took my hand again and led me into her bedroom.

I trembled with nervous anticipation as I removed my shoes. But it felt good and I didn't try to stop it.

"You're shaking," she said, lying down next to me.

"I know," I said, propping myself up on an elbow to embrace her.

"It's okay. I like it," she said, moving on top of me. She sat up and crossed her arms to remove her T-shirt. The straps of her lace bra dug into the flesh of her shoulders and she straddled my hips and leaned over to kiss me. I pointedly decided not to go for her breasts right away, so as not to come off too shallow, but she sat back up and placed my hands on the generous cups of her bra and reached behind her and the straps dug into her shoulders again and she unleashed her breasts into my hands. She squeezed my hands and moaned, clenching her eyes shut as she fell forward. I pressed my lips against the nape of her neck, dropping kisses along her collarbone, trying to do all of the things I imagined Dominic not spending a lot of time on. After the last articles of clothing were discarded, she dug her fingers into my hair, moaning loud and deep and I closed my eyes and breathed in the soft flowers of her neck and hair. I felt as though we were falling.

I reached under and cupped her shoulders and our chests rocked back and forth and it had been so long and she pressed her lips against my ear sending waves down my spine and encouraging me to hold her tighter and I did and her hips bobbed wild and erratic against me and I figured she could fake one at least as good as Meg Ryan, but it didn't matter, as I felt like she was putting on a show just for me and all that she asked in return was my admiration and I think I held up my end of the deal.

She didn't wake up when I pulled back the comforter and admired the soft tones of her face and body in the muted light of the room. She turned on her side, splaying her fingers across her waist, lying still as a painting. And looking at her, it truly *was* a mystery to me that Sharon Stone was in the movies while she was answering phones and Chance with a capital fucking C appeared to be the only element that could possibly be responsibile.

The beer had worn off long ago and I wasn't feeling too bad, although I had a drink on my mind. The plastic cap of the Bic pen in my pocket—I always carry one just in case—jabbed my leg with each step. I stopped in front of a bar. The windows were clouded and I couldn't see inside, but I could feel that odd tractor beam zap through my chest and hook onto my shoulder blades, beckoning me to enter. I stepped inside, but the warmth felt strange and I snatched one of those cardboard triangle beer advertisements off the top of an empty table and walked out. My head spun in an uncomfortable fashion converse to the nausea that used to occur after drinking too much. But I picked up my pace and walked through it, bowing my head as I descended several streets into the stairs of the 9th street PATH entrance, passing my dollar bill through the turnstile as the train pulled away. I sat down on the wooden bench—the only soul on the platform save a burly man working a circular power cleaner.

In the din of his machine, I undid the seam of the advertisement, the back of which provided a sturdy page. I recollected my evening with Dominic and Ernie and Albert and their Courtney Love death bet and the hapless Yankees, but my thoughts dwelled on Grace. I decided that if we had met as characters in a book or a movie, we wouldn't have slept together. Our conversation alone would have provided the necessary double-vision from which to examine my situation. But this was real life. And in real life, people finish their drinks and fuck; Holden Caulfield never existed.

I uncapped my Bic, accidentally elbowing a half-full quart of Colt 45. The warbling bottle rolled towards the tracks, spilling its contents in a haphazard puddle over the freshly buffed platform before falling onto the tracks. My mind was reeling and I relegated Grace to the back of my head, as I pressed down on the pen and began to write.

The Big Game

Did your father ever...hit you?" he asked, rolling his chair back beneath a wallful of diplomas lettered in calligraphy too fancy to read.

"What? Like on a regular basis?"

The shrink recrossed his legs and glanced down at his pad.

"Did he *strike* you?"

"When I fucked up, he gave it to me. You know. He gave it to me pretty good."

"And how often did this occur."

"Mondays, Wednesdays and Fridays at 3," I said, rolling my eyes.

"I'd appreciate it if you would try to take this seriously." The shrink flipped a few pages. "Did he beat you on a regular basis?"

"I *told* you. He beat me whenever I fucked up. And yes, I was always in the process of fucking up. So, yeah."

The shrink let out a dry sigh. Like a man in need of a drink.

"Why don't we talk about when you first started experiencing the feelings you mentioned."

I knew I had to give him something or I'd never get out of there. "I guess I remember when I was about twelve," I said, stopping to test his reaction. "And we were building a clubhouse and this real asshole of a kid stepped through the door and was whining his usual shit and I was gripping a brand new hammer and I had this sudden urge to bury the claw in his head."

The shrink sat up.

"I must have thought about it for like five seconds while I was staring at the back of his neck. I remember because he had one of those haircuts that's shaved all the way up past the ears and it was a fresh cut and real neat and I stared at that clean soft spot right beneath his scalp and I felt the heft of the hammer in my hand and it had a soft black coating and I remember wondering if I could take him out in a single shot. Then somebody called my name and the hammer felt strange and my hand felt weak."

"Like, I wasn't even worried about getting in trouble. And even though I didn't want him to be part of our clubhouse, I wasn't out to maim or kill the bastard. I felt this like electricity pumping through me and I just wanted to sink the claw into that smooth little crater in the back of his head. It was like...the hammer and his head were just objects, existing on their own and I was just...I don't know...curious?" What the fuck are you supposed to tell these guys? "Look, I just had this sudden urge to do it and that's it."

He sat back in his chair. "And the manifestation of these compulsions continued throughout your adolescence?"

I sighed and stared at the dumb ass.

"Tell me again what it feels like when you get these impulses."

Jesus. "On the inside I get cold, but on the outside it feels like someone's cranked up the heat about thirty degrees and my hearing is on like, half-power until it passes."

He sat forward again. Christ, he was eating it up.

"Did you fight a lot with siblings or class mates?"

"I don't have any brothers or sisters. But I fought in the playground like everyone else."

"But this is just play-fighting, no?"

"Yeah, you know, nothing major. Bloody noses, black eyes, split lips. They made you shake afterwards and you squeezed the other guy's hand as hard as you could and that was that."

He stared at me. "What about high school?"

"In my freshman year I started getting into a lot of fights. I was only like five-two—I'm still only five-seven—but I could kick ass for my size. You know, when you're a freshman a lot of the upper-classmen get off on humiliating you in front of chicks. And since I was on the smaller side I got it quite a bit and I guess it was supposed to be fun, but it's not really a joke when it's always you at the butt-end. Anyway there was this one bastard who busted my balls on a regular basis, knocking my books out and pushing me down stairs, and just generally riding me and I sucked it up like everyone else. Then one day, I was standing in the hallway in my gym shorts, bent over at the water fountain and Mr. Asshole comes up behind me and yanks my shorts down to my ankles. He pointed at me and I froze, standing there in my little tightey-whites and there were these upper-classmen girls there and they were laughing at me too, and my face felt like it was on fire. Asshole was hunched over laughing and I yanked up my shorts and charged him, smashing his head sideways against the lockers. *Bam!* Knowing that his head produced the sound it did against the lockers was very satisfying. He went down hard and I pounded his face like I was on automatic pilot until I was pulled off him. I fucked up his face real good and nobody was laughing anymore. Shit like that happened all the time because I guess I looked like an easy target. I went for the throat and landed my knee in their nuts until they lost their shit and then I'd pound the crap out of them like a mad dog until somebody pulled me off. It caught everyone by surprise—even the people standing around. Because, even if a guy's a lot bigger than you, if you can just absorb a few punches and get to his throat and fuck with his Adam's Apple, he'll lose his shit instantly. But the thing was, I never ever picked a fight in my life—and that's the honest-to-God truth. But there are plenty of other guys who will. It doesn't take much. Some guy at a party thinks he's all pumped up and locks his shoulders forward as he walks through a crowded room—that sort of thing.

"And I swear to you on my mother's grave, I never ever attacked a girl before. I mean I've *wanted* to lots of times, you know, the prick-teasers who like to play head-games and give you blue-balls. There've been lots of girls who *could've* used a good crack here and there, but I never felt the *urge* to do it."

"Well this girl was certainly not, as you say, *a prick-teaser.*"

"Certainly not."

The shrink scribbled something on a pad.

"Look! I don't...shit...she's a messed up slut of a chick. I mean, she's got the condoms of every guy she's ever been with hanging from her wall. It looks like a used balloon dart board at a carnival."

"Are you aware of the fact," he sat forward and looked me in the eye like he was going to lay some heavy shit on me. "That when she was ten years old, she was in a car accident that killed her younger brother and both of her parents?" He sat back and folded his hands.

"Yeah I heard something like that, but you know, it's fucked up all around. My mother died of cancer when I was eleven. You know, so I'm sorry. It's a hard fucking world."

"You certainly like profanity, don't you?"

"I talk like everybody else." I said.

The shrink raised his eyebrows.

"Christ Al*mighty*! I watched my mother deteriorate to a fucking skeleton when I was eleven years old! You don't see me making a collection of used fucking maxi-pads on my wall!"

"Take it easy. Take it-"

"Jesus-Fucking-Christ!"

"You're not on trial here."

"Well, that's what it feels like." My heart was pounding. Don't lose your shit, I told myself. That's what he wants. Just say your bit and get out.

The shrink sighed. "Why don't you tell me again about the party you attended."

"Look," I said.

"I was at this party/
This guy started fucking with me/
When he saw I wasn't going to back down/
He let his friends pull him away."

I had told him this so many times, it started to sound like I was reciting the Pledge of Allegiance.

"So I felt the rush and when it didn't happen, it gave me kind of a headache and I went back to my dorm. Ten minutes later she comes down the hall and picks me out. I hadn't gotten any in awhile and whenever you go to parties there's always tons of chicks dressed real slutty. So, you know, I was good to go."

"And you had been drinking."

"Not really. I had maybe nine beers. So I get up to her room and she closes her door and starts undressing and I checked out her wall to see how many of my friends were actually telling the truth. Anyway, she's completely naked and she starts playing with herself and I'm like, *that's pretty cool,* because I had never seen a woman do that, but then I was like, well what the fuck do you need me for? So anyway I'm finally fucking her and after awhile she starts yelling, Harder, fuck me harder! and I start really pounding into her, like full-force and she's humping her hips up into me and she keeps screaming, HARDER! and like I couldn't possibly fuck her any harder than I was, I mean I'm already pounding the crap out of her and then her hips drop and she's like whatever and just stares at the wall after getting me all going and like I don't even *remember* touching her throat and I'm telling you, it's pure bullshit."

I had the shrink on the edge of his chair.

"So then she starts like clawing my hands and it fucking hurt and then the rush came over me and I guess I grabbed her throat too hard."

He raised his eyebrows. "Were you oblivious to the consequences of...grabbing her throat too hard?"

"I don't know...yeah, whatever."

"Please try and think. Did you ever consider her welfare or any possible repercussions resulting from your actions?"

"Christ, I don't know." I rolled back my sleeve. "Look isn't it time yet?"

"I suppose."

"When do I have to come back?"

"Every Monday and Thursday at 4."

Shit, I thought, this is as bad as having a sixth class—except I'm not getting any credits.

"And how long do we do this?"

"As long as it takes. Or until the end of the semester."

"Alright, so...what do you want to know for next time?"

"Whether or not you were aware of the consequences of your actions."

"The consequences of my actions. Alright. Let's see if we

can take care of that next week. Goodbye." I closed the door and sped down the hall, hoping I wouldn't run into anyone I knew and hoping I could get back to the Desert before they cleaned up dinner, but I knew I'd probably just miss it, thanks to the cocksuckers over at the Department of Residential Life. They really lowered the boom. I mean, what the fuck? It was her word against mine. And someone as fucked up and slutty as her should have a little less credibility. Plus she's totally exaggerating. I touch her throat and she goes ape-shit and this fucking PC campus buys the whole thing hook, line and sinker. I mean did any of those people ever stop for a second and think that I would have to explain this to my father? No. Thank God my mother isn't alive to hear it. Christ, you think relocating me to the Desert would be enough. But to be honest, I didn't mind relocation too much because some people were starting to give me evil looks in the dorm. A few times I had eaten dinner all by myself real fast just so I could get back up to my room. At least in my new dorm, the dining room is huge, so it's not a problem. Still, I knew someone would eventually hear about the whole thing and these guys asked me about it and I was like, awww fuck...but then one of them told me how he fucked this girl and she was really bombed and like even though she had fucked all these other guys, they still charged him with date-rape. I could totally see it happening, too. And the other guys were like, yeah, DRL fucking sucks and Gample sucks and like they didn't make a big deal about it at all and I've been hanging around with them a lot.

They also put me on probation. Whatever. And then forty hours of community service. When I first heard this, I imagined myself in a white apron behind a counter ladling out soup to a bunch of crackheads in Willirico. But you know what they make me do? I have to help out the janitor for an hour every morning. But the guy's way cool. He's this little

Mexican guy named Benny, who tokes up all the time and half the time he just tells me "Heyyy, *my friend!* Today you sleep!" So I go back to my room and grab another hour. Sometimes after party nights, I pick up the empties in the hallway and sweep the stairs for him and I don't mind at all because he's such a cool fucking guy.

But DRL really knows how to throw the book at you. This one woman thought I was an alcoholic and wanted me to do some kind of program, but she's black and I heard she's a dyke and she hates white guys and she tries to do that with everyone who's drunk when they get in trouble. I mean who are these fucking people? If I *was* as fucked up as they were making me out to be, I don't see how moving me out of the dorm and cleaning the floors was supposed to "rehabilitate" me. They're so full of shit. Those cunts just wanted to punish me. And you know these are the same bleeding hearts that say the death penalty is wrong. Bunch of fucking fascist P.C. bull-dykes. But what's done is done. No point crying over spilled milk. I just have to figure out how to get that shrink off my ass.

It was Thursday—the biggest party night of the week. I actually considered going to my six o'clock, but some of the guys I started hanging around with in my new dorm were starting early for the Big Game and then heading over to Jeb's. I *should* go. I mean they've been wicked cool to me. People were lined up around the Pavilion and I forgot about the shrink and thought about the Big Game. Everyone will be out partying. The bars will be crowded.

* * *

"My-mother-died-of-cancer-when-I-was-eleven blah blah BLAH!" These fucking kids get more miserable every year, I thought, eyeing my Ph.D. hanging on the wall over the waste

basket in the corner of my office.

I debated whether or not to pour a second drink as I looked over my schedule. Just a five o'clock and then home for the Big Game. I was almost glad Terry didn't offer his season tickets. I decided to grab a twelve-pack at Jeb's on the way home and just relax in front of the TV.

My secretary buzzed me: "Virginia Reynard on line 1."

Christ Almighty. I reached for the phone. "Do you think the secretary is an idiot?"

"He's not coming home tonight," she said.

I emptied my lungs of smoke and stubbed out my cigarette. Virginia was married to this sexless Jesus-freak who ran the foreign language lounge, and we had been keeping company with one another since my wife left. I was already set on unwinding in front of the Big Game. I didn't know what to say.

"He said he was working late at the language lounge. I just called him back but there was no answer. I've already found a sitter..." She always knew what tone to assume.

"I don't want to miss the Big Game," I told her.

"We could watch it together," she purred.

"Okay." I poured another medium glass of Red Label and flashed on drawing my pension in five years. "Why don't you come by after half-time."

"When is that?"

"Around nine-thirty," I said.

"Okay," she sighed expectantly.

"Will you be dressed for the occasion?"

"I already am." She hung up and I downed my scotch in two gulps. Who am I kidding, I thought, knowing full well my secretary already knows the score. I glanced at the picture of my ex-wife and wondered if she still thinks about me from time to time. I took a double-shot of Binaca before replacing the bottle of Red Label in the defunct umbrella holder in the far corner of my closet. I drained my tepid coffee and set the clock on my wall five minutes ahead and buzzed my secretary to send in my five-thirty.

¡No Mas!

George was curled up in the passenger seat with a line of drool connecting his chin to his flowered shirt. The intro to Zeppelin's *In My Time of Dying* crawled across the radio and I cranked it up and whacked myself in the face to stay awake. George never woke up. It's a good thing that in California they got those round things embedded in the road to keep you in your lane on the freeway, because more than once my head jerked up to the *rrwwwumppp! rrwwwumppp!* of George's Chevette drifting out of its lane. If I was driving back home on the narrow lanes of the Parkway, we'd probably be dead by now.

rrwwumppp! rrwwwumppp!

My chin popped up and I was straddling the middle lane on Route 5. Fuckin-A I just wanted to get back up to L.A. and get some sleep. I rolled the window all the way down and whacked myself again. The tequila wasn't helping me stay alert either, but my lousy driving wasn't because I drank too much. I was just tired, that's all. And I was tired of our vacation. The prospect of beginning our drive all the way back to Jersey the next morning didn't thrill me either. I just wanted to be back in my house in Lodensack lying next to my wife in my own bed.

I had never been to Mexico. When George suggested we go to Tijuana, I said sure. It caught me by surprise because being from the East Coast, I never thought of Mexico as being beneath California. I only thought of it as being south of Texas. But geography wasn't my best subject. So anyways, I was pretty excited because when Georgie said Mexico, I imagined pretty women with silky hair dressed in white and dancing with those snapping things in their hands, while men in white suits and red sashes played guitars and blew trumpets from under sombreros. I thought of Brando in *Viva Zapata!* and honor and bullfights and tortillas and tequila. But Mexico wasn't like that at all. The only thing they had was the tequila and it tasted like crap. Tijuana was a shithole and the Mexicans were a bunch of dirty hawkers and whores that weren't even women—all of them the most dishonest fuckers I ever laid eyes on.

We arrived at the border just as the sun went down. All of the parking lots on the U.S. side had a maximum charge of five or six bucks. George didn't like the looks of the attendants and since we had all our stuff in the car, for a few dollars more, we parked the car in the nicest lot, that was well lit and all. Georgie's smart about stuff like that. We walked up a ramp that looked like a parking garage to cross the border on foot and we stopped halfway across the fenced overpass to look at the lines of cars waiting to get into Mexico and it stretched back further than we could see and we figured since it was Friday, everyone was headed to

Tijuana for a good time. We went down some steps and passed through one of those one way revolving doors with thick bars and we were in Mexico and at the end of the stretch all these guys asked us if we wanted a taxi. George ignored them but they kept asking and he shook his head and said "No, Grassy-ass!" and it seemed to work. We walked over towards a big yellow Tecate sign and we passed some booths but it looked pretty dead.

"I'm thirsty," I said.

"Awright," George said.

We started towards this little strip of outdoor cafes and these guys came up to us and started trying to get us to sit down at their places. George ignored them and asked a waiter how much was a beer. The waiter said ninety cents and George ordered two beers and we sat down and he struck up a conversation with the white people at the next table.

"It's pretty dead here, huh?" George said.

They laughed and then this guy said, "I think you're looking for the Avenue Revolooseyown."

"Do you have to take a cab?" George asked.

The guy shook his head and pointed at another ramp. "Just follow the crowd."

The waiter set down two Corona bottles and folded his arms. I took a big sip and George raised his bottle. The waiter asked for two dollars.

"You told me a beer was ninety cents," George said.

The guy at the other table smiled.

"Ninety cents Mexican beer," the waiter said.

"Corona *is* Mexican beer," George said.

The waiter shook his head no.

"I didn't *ask* for a Corona. I asked for a *beer*. And you said it was ninety cents."

"Mexican beer ninety cents. Corona, one dollar."

"Come on, George," I said. "It's a fuckin dime for Chrissakes."

George shot me one of his looks as I pulled out two dollars. He grabbed it from my hands and handed it to the waiter. "Your tip's included," he said and turned back to me. "I know a dime aint jack shit, but it's the fucking *principle.* You don't speak up and these people'll take you for everything you got."

Whatever. I wanted to get to the Revolooseyown so I gulped my beer knowing George wouldn't want me to finish too far ahead of him. I just wanted to get fucked up.

We walked through the covered ramp and when we stepped out, the sky had gone from purple to charcoal black and we passed all these busted up tin-roofed shacks with people peddling gigantic plastic chili peppers and all this other bullshit and I was getting good at saying "No, Grassy-ass!" and then I saw the street sign: Avenue Revolucion.

We turned left and the sidewalk was littered with fluorescent pieces of paper that chicks in hot pants with different shades of bleached orange hair were handing out trying to get you inside. Some bars had as many as five hawkers hanging outside trying to rope you in. I was kind of disappointed at the selection—there wasn't one—it was all clubs with flashing lights, blaring that thumping techno crap out onto the street. I stopped to eye one of the chicks and George grabbed my arm. "Come on. Let's find a *bar* bar."

We walked down the street, but all we found were clubs.

"Don't they have any bars that play music that has fucking *instruments* in it?" George joked. But he was right; it was shitty music, shitty atmosphere and shitty looking guys hanging out the doors. Fucking clubs. It was like, this place is trying way too hard to be all the things I *dislike* about American nightlife. Some guy grabbed my arm and told us beers were 75 cents.

"Let's go in," I said. "All of em are playing techno."

George nodded and the guy led us in. There were only a dozen people in the whole place and the guy sat us at this table pretty far from everyone else and whipped out a pad.

"How much did you say beer was?" George asked him.

The man looked at the ceiling and then said, "75 cents."

"Two beers," George said.

The man looked at me like he couldn't hear George over the thump of the music and I said, "TWO BEERS!"

He nodded and walked off and then George went to take a leak. The man returned with four uncapped bottles on a tray.

"No," I put a hand up. "I said *two*."

The guy nodded real fast and gripped two of the bottles in his fist and set them up in front of me.

"No!" I replaced two of the bottles on his tray. "TWO! Not four. Two. *Dos*!" I remembered that one from Sesame Street.

"You drink one now and then another beer!" he exclaimed, attempting to smooth over my pissed-offness with his house party tone and a wave of his hand.

I stood up like I was going to leave.

"Okay." The man took back two of the bottles and I pulled out two singles. "Two dollars," he said.

"You said 75 cents!" Jesus-Fucking-Christ-Almighty these people.

"You pay. The bottle," he mumbled some kind of bullshit.

"Fuck that," I said, standing again.

"Okayyyyyy!" He took the two dollars and pulled out a handful of coins and pushed aside the quarters and poked five dimes onto the table. What a dumb fucker. If he just said a dollar-fifty from the start, I would have just *given* him the two dollars. George turned out of the bathroom, pulling his zipper and I told him what happened.

"That figures," he said.

Behind George, one of the bartenders grabbed the wrist of this blond chick and helped her up onto the bar. She did that stupid fucking Arsenio Hall woof-woof fist crank and started dancing. The guy cranked the music up even more—God it was fucking horrible. You think people'd hit a boiling point when they just can't take any more of that artificial bullshit and they'd want real music played by human fucking beings instead of this Euro-fucking-Sprockets crap that everyone open-throats like a bunch of starving baby birds. But the chick on the bar started dancing real hard and one of the bartenders started doing pelvic thrusts and then the chick started doing pelvic thrusts like it was a game of Simon Says. This group of five guys with buzzcuts outside on the sidewalk stopped to check her out through the glass and she really started humping the air. Then the guy who roped us in was outside working the buzzcuts. 30 seconds later he sat them down at a table in front of the chick dancing on the bar and brought them over a bucket of uncapped beers. The chick was bucking her meaty ass back and forth and I grabbed my bottle but it was empty. This other American chick came running up to the bartender and pointed at the bar. The bartender helped her up and then three more guys sat down and then two more chicks saw the group of guys and started dancing near the bar and in like two minutes, the place went from near desertion to a steady crowd. I dreamt about opening up my own place back in Lodensack until the bartender came back to our table. He wanted to sell us a bucket of six beers for three dollars.

"Let's do it up, George," I said, eyeing the first chick.

"You really think after all that bullshit, this guy's going to be honest?"

"Even if we get em for four-"

"Fuck that. Let's go."

"But George, they-"

"Don't worry, there's going to be tits and ass everywhere."

"Awright."

We walked out and came upon this one bar that had those poles with the thick red ropes that they use to keep you in line at the movies, except no one was on line.

"Two beer two tequila three dollar!"

George looked at the guy. "So you get two beers, two-"

"Two beer two tequila three dollar!"

"Like a broken fucking record," George said to me. "Let's do it."

A thin layer of sawdust covered the floor and it was pretty crowded inside. The guy cleared a spot at the bar and set up two long necks and George asked the guy again, "Two beers and two tequilas for three dollars?"

He nodded and George passed three singles over the bar and this other guy came up behind George and then someone grabbed my forehead from behind, restraining me. I tried to reach behind me and a Cuervo bottle floated over my head with a red pourer and my mouth was filled and out of the corner of my eye I saw that George, with a Newport still burning between his fingers, was being served his tequila in the same way. So I relaxed and swallowed but it was watered down or something because if somebody filled your entire mouth with Cuervo and you swallowed, you'd fuckin know about it. I was handed my beer as though I needed a chaser, which I didn't and then I was grabbed again from behind and my face was wiped with a rag. Before I could turn around, they did the whole thing over again and when the guy wiped my face down a second time, he was twisting my neck and fucking with my hair and I was ready to put that greaseball to sleep, but I kept cool because it was a local thing and I guess it was supposed to be fun. I looked over at George smiling and I raised my beer and then one of the guys said, "seeks dollars."

"Don't give me that fucking bullshit!" George slammed his bottle down on the counter and foam rose up the neck. "You said three dollars for two beers and two tequilas and I *fucking* paid you!"

The bartender pointed at two plastic shot glasses filled with a pale yellow liquid. They looked like two piss tests.

"Two beer, two tequila, three dollars." The bartender chopped the air with his hand to signal that part had been settled. "Poppers, six dollars. You pay." He smacked the bar.

I sighed and reached for the tequila shot.

"Don't fucking drink that!" George pointed at me. "Take those tequilas back!" he said to the bartender. "There's your fucking payment!" He grabbed my arm for us to leave and this guy in a blue suit stood in front of us and folded his arms. He was only like five-six but he was built like a hard-on and most definitely could've kicked my ass. He had light hair for a Mexican and he looked kind of like Marky-Mark.

"You pay," he said, "Or I call the police."

"Go call the fucking police!" George said.

Marky-Mark shrugged and unhooked a walkie-talkie and mumbled something in Spanish. George gave his back and raised his beer and I did the same. Marky-Mark leaned over my shoulder from behind. "You pay! Or you come with me!" I could feel his hot breath in my ear but I ignored him. But when I felt him grab my arm, I spun around and ripped his hand off.

"KEEP YOUR FUCKING HANDS OFF ME COCKSUCKER!" I screamed in his face. I could feel my whole body trembling, and I was praying to God he wouldn't do anything. He backed off a step.

"Where's the fucking police?!" My face felt hot.

"Me," he stuck a thumb against a badge on his breast. "Police."

"You're not the *police*!" George pointed a finger into his

badge that said SECURITY in big letters. "You're a fucking *security* guard!"

Marky-Mark's face got red and he reached behind him and pulled out a pair of black handcuffs. "You come with me!" He was fuming.

"Fuck you," George said.

One of the bartenders stepped between them and asked what was the problem and my heart was pounding as I flashed on horror stories of torture and well-fed rats in cold Mexican prisons and I explained the whole thing, telling him we never asked for the poppers and we didn't drink the tequila shots and he patted my chest and nodded and said "It's OK. No problem. You pay *seecks dollors*."

Mother*fucker,* these guys. A lot of tourists had stopped dancing and crowded around and I felt more confident. "No, you get the police," I told him and gave them my back and took a nursing sip of my beer, glancing at Marky-Mark and all the tourists eyeing him. His face got redder until he looked like he was ready to blast off.

"Are the police here yet?" George asked him all cutesy-like, as though he were mouthing off to the school bully while clinging to the teacher's dress. He can be a real asshole when he wants to be. One of the managers went over and said something to Marky-Mark in Spanish and Marky-Mark started to talk back but the guy cut him off. Marky-Mark mumbled into his walkie-talkie and then held it to his ear and nodded and said "See!" He shot George a murderous look and then bolted up the stairs. The bartender took back the tequila shots and told us we could go and we got the fuck out of there.

My head was spinning on the sidewalk and I wanted more alcohol in a big way. We came upon this one bar that had a balcony and we could see it was all Americans and the guy at the door said, "One beer 75 cent."

"Yeah and the Pope sucks dick," Georgie said, as we followed the guy inside.

It looked a little less crazy on the balcony and I asked the guy if we could sit out there and he nodded and led us inside and a big white sign said DRAFT BEER 75¢ BOTTLE $1.50. George looked at me and I ordered two draft beers just because. They tasted like piss.

At the table next to us, three young guys with buzzcuts were pulling beer bottles out of a white spackle bucket. It seemed like two thirds of the American guys in Tijuana had buzz cuts. Four shots of tequila sat on their table. George pointed at the shots and asked them how much they were.

"You guys can have em," one of them said in a Southern accent.

We downed the shots and George asked them where they were from.

"I'm from Texas and he's from Virginia and he's from Florida," Texas said, pointing out the others, "but we all live in San Diego."

George told him how we were from Jersey and had taken a road trip cross country to visit a guy in L.A. who used to work at the Water Company.

"New Jersey," Texas said. "I knew it was either there or New York."

"How'd you know that," I asked him.

"From your accents."

"Our accents?"

That cracked me up because people in New Jersey talk like everyone else. Like the way people talk on TV. This guy sounded like the Beverly Fucking Hillbillies and he's telling us we have accents. I could tell by the look on George's face he was thinking the same thing but he let it go. They did give us four tequilas. George asked them what they do and Virginia piped up and said they were all in seal training.

"*Really*," George said. He looked impressed.

"That must be a lot of fun," I said.

Florida looked at me kind of funny and then George glared at me. I finished my beer and then faced Texas. "So did you have to go to veterinarian school or something?"

Florida looked pissed, Virginia looked confused and Texas started laughing. George gave me one of his looks. This was his 'Sometimes It Blows My Mind How Fucking Stupid You Are' look. Florida went off to take a leak.

"What?" I said.

"They're not seal trainers, they're *Navy* SEALs."

"What's that?"

George leaned into me and whispered, "*Do you realize how fucking hard-core these guys are?* They could kill you in six seconds and you wouldn't even make a sound." He downed another one of the tequilas and smacked the empty shot upside-down on the table and nodded at them.

Whatever, you know. I didn't think it was that stupid of me. I mean there *is* a zoo in San Diego and they *do* have seals.

The SEALs pulled the last beers from their bucket.

"I remember when they brought you guys out in Panama," George said. "Fuckin-A."

Virginia nodded. "Yeah. Five guys got killed." He said it like it was supposed to back up how heavy duty they were, but that didn't sound very impressive to me. But I didn't know about shit like that. George did. Sometimes I wish I never dropped out of J.C.

Florida came back and told us that they had a mechanical bull going for free.

"Let's do it," George said, all enthusiastic-like even though he would never in a million years get on a mechanical bull. The SEALs looked pretty gung-ho and we followed them. I had never really seen a mechanical bull except for *Urban Cowboy*.

There was a short line and the SEALs rushed over to get on the end of it. They waved George over.

"I can't," George said, patting an imaginary injury on his knee, "I been on the D-L since high school."

They looked at me and I looked at George and shook my head and I got on line with the SEALs. The bull was cranking and it tossed this guy and he landed kind of on his shoulder and I suddenly remembered a thing I saw on TV about a guy who used to be able to do 20 pushups with one arm until he fell off a mechanical bull and then he couldn't even lift himself.

This blond chick got on. She had quite a rack on her and she hiked up her bluejean miniskirt and reached down between her legs to grab the thing you hold on to. The Mexican guy working the controls made the bull go real slow in a circle and her body rose and fell and her tits were bouncing all over the place and when the bull dropped she sat up straight and her tits pushed out and it was fucking better than *Baywatch*. The SEALs started cheering and the zipper in back of her skirt was starting to come undone and the guy working the controls sped up the bull just for a second and the girl's body jerked and the zipper dropped. Everyone started cheering and she was really getting into it. She had a nice big ass and see-through white lace panties that veiled a tattoo of the American flag on her right asscheek and with her hand buried beneath her fat crotch it looked like she was playing with herself while riding the shit out of the bull. I stuffed my free hand in my pocket and when she got off, the SEALs pounced on her like she was a fucking enemy invader or something. She re-adjusted her miniskirt and then this other buzzcut came over and he looked really pissed and he was pretty put together. I was ready to see just what the

SEALs were supposedly capable of, but the guy grabbed the chick's wrist and pulled her away.

"Fuck it," Texas said. "Let's get another bucket."

"Okay," I said, glad I didn't have to follow the SEALs onto the bull.

We ended up shelling out fifteen bucks for a bucket of ten beers and after doing the math in my head I realized there was absolutely no savings there. I guess you don't have to be a rocket scientist to be a Navy SEAL. But then when the bucket arrived, I saw Virginia had got them to throw in four shots of tequila. We toasted to getting laid or something—I couldn't hear across the techno—and downed the tequila. As we worked on the beers, these pain-in-the-ass waitresses kept coming up to us and asking us if we wanted something to drink and we just kept pointing at the bucket, but this kept happening like every thirty seconds. They wouldn't leave us the fuck alone to drink in peace and they weren't even good-looking or anything. One of them asked me for the third time and I surprised myself again with another little bit of Spanish I knew: "*¡No mas!*"

We went back to the balcony to get the waitresses off our asses, and the bull-riding chick was there standing next to the buzzcut who pulled her away. He gripped a long neck resting on the table, and his other arm was wrapped around the chicks thighs with his hand up inside her bluejean miniskirt, working that American flag in front of everyone and she didn't even give a fuck.

"We gotta drink up tonight," Texas told me. "They got elections and there's no more booze after 12."

"That's fucked," I said.

"Why's that?"

"What does drinking have to do with elections?"

He shook his head and we left the bar and on the crumbling wall in faded red letters someone had spray-painted **¡VIVA COLOSIO!**

"Who's Colosio?" I asked Texas.

He breathed out hard through his nose. "Who gives a fuck," he snarled.

We went to another club and Florida took up a collection.

"We're gonna get two buckets," he said.

We started drinking the buckets and a few minutes later this guy handed us a stack of white styrofoam cups and put a finger over his lips and told us to pour all the beers into the cups so that we don't get in trouble. We poured all the beers and I looked up at the dance floor and leaning against the railing was this really hot Mexican chick. We made eye contact and she smiled and I got up from the table, but George ripped me back down.

"Gimme your wallet," he said.

I slipped it to him under the table and walked over to the chick and asked her to dance. Up close she wasn't as good-looking and she certainly wasn't dressed like how I had imagined the dancing Mexican women. She had all this shit gooped up around her eyes and she wore this black thing that pushed her tits up and out as though she were hanging by her heels. The tip of her tongue appeared between her ruby red lips and then disappeared and when she turned I caught a glimpse of her tight little ass and God*damn*! We started dancing and she didn't stop me when I slid my hands down her hips and she got up on her toes and ground her bush into me and fuckin-A I reached around and gripped her rock-hard ass and asked her how old she was.

"17," she said.

Holy shit. I hadn't touched a 17-year-old since I was like 25. I do have some scruples, you know, but she stood up high to get the top of my pole and fuckin-A I started scoping the place out for a private corner or something or someplace outside but what about George and I tried to kiss her but she wouldn't let me and she humped me again, *hard* and then I reached down for it and I thought I was going to shoot a load right there until I glanced down at the liner pulled out of one of my pockets and her hand in the other one.

"You little fucking bitch!" I said, stepping away and covering my hard-on while tucking my pocket back in. She put this look on her face like I was off my chair and she was really offended, but it didn't matter because nobody saw what happened anyway. But then my heart dropped when I felt my flat pocket. I stepped towards her but then I remembered that George had taken my wallet. And then I noticed this bad-assed Mexican at the door staring right at me with this look like I better chill the fuck out. I grabbed the railing for a second and got my shit together and went back to the table. Virginia and Texas were working these chicks that were old enough to be their mothers. George read the rotten look on my face.

"Would you like your wallet back now?"

I grabbed it from him. It really pissed me off when he did shit like that, but obviously I was glad he did. The Mexican bouncer was still eyeing me.

"Let's get the fuck outta here," I said to George.

"Okay." George told Florida we were taking off.

"Aw, don't go yet," Florida said. "As soon as these two realize they have no chance with the grannies, we'll head over to a strip club."

George said no thanks and drained his cup. Florida kept trying to get us to go along. They were friendly guys, the SEALs, but I had no idea why they wanted to hang out with older guys like George and me to begin with. I braced my hand for bone-crushing handshakes since they were hardcore in the military and all, but their grips were relaxed and we said good-bye.

I was still flying at half-mast and my nuts ached, but it felt good to be outside. As we walked back towards the border, men asked us if we wanted taxis. We said no and then they asked us if we wanted *poo-see*.

"You go off with one of those bastards," George jerked his thumb at them "and you'll be *guaranteed* to get fucked." He slurred his words and was stumbling all over the place and I figured it was probably an unspoken thing that I was going to drive George's Chevette and I wondered if maybe I was too fucked up.

"I'm starving," I said.

"You wanna go to Denny's?" George pointed out the familiar yellow sign. We must have put away five Super Slam breakfasts apiece since we got out West. They don't really have Denny's back in Jersey.

"Awright," I said, thinking a couple cups of coffee would bolt me up for the drive back to our buddy's place in L.A. George tripped over a nonexistent stoop at the entrance and looked down at it like it was somebody else's fault. Georgie's kind of a lightweight and his fucked-upedness was starting to show.

Inside it looked exactly like a Denny's in California, except it wasn't as nice and it was all Mexicans. We sat down at the counter and a woman handed us two greasy menus. I didn't even look at mine and since I wasn't that hungry, I passed on the Super Slam breakfast for the Grand Slam.

"Wait a minute!" George jabbed his finger into the menu. All of the prices were in pesos. "How much is this in American dollars?" The whole counter heard him.

The woman walked over to the register and then back.

"Three-fifty-six," she said.

"*Three-fifty-six!?* It's only a dollar ninety-nine in the *United* STATES!" George slurred his words real slow.

"Come on." He grabbed my arm. "Let's...get...outta here. Let's get out of this country."

Fuckin-A. At bare minimum I needed a few cupsa joe for the ride home and I wasn't going to get them because of

George and his fucking principles.

"Let's get the fuck outta this dumphole," George half sang as we swerved down the Avenue Revolucion following the arrows for the border until two whores approached us.

"Awright," George bent over and broke into a silent laughing fit. "Gimme your wallet again."

One of the whores started walking alongside me. She was tall and had a nice big set of legs on her and she put her arm around my waist and I got rock fucking hard again. It was like my seventh boner of the night. The other one put her arm around George and he put a hand on his wallet and gave me a look like we'll just fuck with them until we get to the corner. Mine kept offering to suck me off for twelve dollars and she started rubbing my johnson and when I looked over I saw George was getting the same treatment.

Georgie dropped back and I moved ahead some and she kept rubbing me and coming on to me in her raspy voice, trying to get me to go with her and after all of the trim I'd been eyeballing and rubbing up against all night, I just couldn't take it anymore so I grabbed her wrist and pressed down and shot a load in my shorts.

"Ohhhh," she groaned at the loss of her business prospect. I could fucking care less. George caught up to me and he had a stupid smile on his face.

"Fuck them!" George sang. "Let's get the fuck outta here."

Georgie lost his balance and caught his right shoulder on a doorway and the whores passed us, switching their asses fast and hard. The ass on mine wasn't that great—not heart shaped at all—it even got skinnier as it went down—holy fuckin shit—I checked out the ass on George's and it was the same and my eyes shot up to the shoulders and they were as broad as mine. The load in my shorts suddenly felt like hot grainy diarrhea and my heart stopped.

"George!" My voice came out in a falsetto. "Those are fucking men!"

"What duh fuckerya talkin abou'?" he mumbled with half-closed eyes.

The whores turned around and their thick brows and bobbing Adam's apples were as good as DNA. Georgie went bug-eyed and his face lost its color like he was gonna deliver a street pizza.

"YOU FUCKING QUEERS!" he screamed at them.

"YOU DIRTY FUCKING...*FAGGOTS*!" He charged the one who rubbed him but it put up its arms and sent George on his ass. Its voice cracked and then grew husky and its screaming went from English into Spanish like fucking Ricky Riccardo when he got pissed at Lucy and George was trying to get up and calling it a faggot and then it started crying and ran over to George and so did I because even though it was a fairy in a skirt, the bottom line was a fairly large Mexican man was stepping up to kick George's drunken ass.

I got between them and apologized for George and said he was drunk and all and it wiped its cheeks with a purple tissue and I felt like a pussy for having to stand there and be all diplomatic with a deceptive fucking faggot who's ass I would have liked to've kicked myself Jesus-Fucking-Christ I just wanted to get out of there. The fucking mutant senoritas sped off and when I looked over at George, his face was white and a line of puke ran from his chin to a thin golden deposit on the sidewalk. His Newports fell out of his shirt pocket into the puke and he snatched them up with a quickness that didn't seem possible considering how fucked up he was.

"Fuck!" he said, dragging his cuff across his mouth.

"Come on. Let's just go." I helped him up, but his legs were only on half-power until he was able to get an arm around me. He took deep breaths and seemed to be getting his shit back together. "Jesus-Christ-fucking-queers," he moaned.

"George?"

"What?"

I had to ask him.

"You didn't shoot a load, did you?"

"NO!" His eyebrows shot up and his mouth opened wide as though I just asked him the most outrageous question of his life. "Djou?"

"Yeah, right..." I mumbled, hoping he wouldn't glance down at my pants.

We stumbled through customs and I took out my drivers license but the guy saw we weren't Mexican and waved us through the turnstile. When we got to the car I checked it out and nothing was stolen. George slumped over the car with his eyes closed, holding onto the handle until I opened his door. He fell inside and I looked at my watch and figured the parking was going to cost eight bucks. I had to walk around to close Georgie's door and I fumbled with the keys until I got everything to work right. I pulled up to the booth, my arm hanging out the window, clutching a five, three ones and the ticket.

"Nine dollars," the guy said.

Christ Almighty.

"Isn't it eight dollars?" I said.

"Nine dollars."

My head dropped on my shoulder. "These motherfucking people don't quit," I said to George but he was already out. I jolted the car forward three feet and examined the rates in my sideview mirror. The guy was actually right. I *did* owe him nine bucks. It took me three tries to put the car in reverse and I jammed the car back and stepped on the brake, rocking to a stop.

I held out a ten for the guy. He took the ten and then the weirdest thing happened: the guy peeled off three singles for my change.

Now, one thing I've always prided myself on was that if I found a wallet full of money, or if someone gives me back too much change, I always return it. Just a little thing I do to help grease my way into Heaven. But when I glanced back at the Mexican guy punching the register, I thought about everyone trying to rip us off and I looked back at the singles and stuffed them under my crotch and pulled the fuck out of there.

On the road, I came upon a yellow sign like they have for animal crossings, except it had a black outline of a Mexican family dashing across the highway. I thought it was pretty fucking hilarious and I nudged George but he was dead. I guess it made sense they'd have a sign like that. If I had to live in that dump, I'd bust out too. I wondered if those people ever felt like God cheated them. I mean it's just a question of a few miles—they happened to pop out on the other side of the line. I couldn't help thinking that maybe God loved me a little more and made me American. And those people must think it too. How else do they account for the fact that they're stuck in that miserable fucking country? My eyes felt heavy and I cranked up the radio and whacked myself in the face and felt lucky to be American.

The car in front of me put its hand in front of the rearview mirror and I backed off. Christ, I was tired. And I was dreading the drive all the way back to Jersey. I missed my wife. I thought about lying next to her in bed with her back to me and my arms around her as I kissed the back of her neck. I don't know why, but whenever I miss my wife, I think about kissing the back of her neck. She's an angel. A fucking angel. And she deserves much better than a shithead like me. I shifted in my seat as the guilt set in about my run-in with the girl who tried to rip me off. What the fuck was I thinking? I wondered if I would have gone with her and I told myself that I wouldn't have, but in the back of my head, I knew how these things worked and I started to feel worse. God, I'm such a shit-for-brains. I mean what the fuck am I doing? I'm never going to strike it rich or do anything different. I'm just going to get older, and I can't keep doing this same stupid fucking bullshit. My heart ached for my wife. I just wanted to get back home to Lodensack. I pressed down on my armrest and lifted my ass off the seat but I still couldn't get comfortable. I leaned to the right and stole a glance at myself in the rearview mirror. I looked like hell. The whites of my eyes were bloodshot and yellow and bags the color of dirt hung beneath them. I ducked my forehead beneath the mirror and stared up at the red glow spreading across the edge of the sky in the East, and for some reason I thought about my brother and suddenly, I wanted children. And it was the first time since I got married that I wanted them unconditionally. My wife's been wanting to get pregnant more than anything and I've been such an asshole. I'll get tested, I decided. Maybe there is something the doctors can do. I'll do whatever it takes. I didn't care how fucked up the world was anymore. Hell, maybe my kids'll be the ones who'll save it. They'll be smart and play sports and go to college and fly airplanes and *rrwwummppp! rrwwumpppp!*

My chin snapped up from my chest and my eyes popped open at the sound of the tires drifting into the next lane. Red splotches seeped across the sky as if the sunrise was on fast-forward. The radio was playing two stations at the same time, one passing, one coming and I turned up the hellish noise and whacked myself again in the face. Christ, I was tired.

The Last Pilgrimage of the 20th Century

GET IN THE GODDAMNED CAR!" I screamed at Billy, chasing him across the Motel 6 parking lot towards the Chevy wagon. I drew a deep breath, examining my squashed reflection in the side window above the wood paneling and patted down the cowlicks that had overcome a generous application of Brill Cream.

"We haven't gone to the San Diego-" Jenny whined

"We don't have time for the zoo," I said.

"But you promised!"

"Shut up!"

Boy, kids today. When I was their age, I would have given my right arm to see something like this. My own father never shut up about how he was at Times Square for V-J Day, and now, finally, I get to see something that will grace the pages of history books until the end of time.

"Can't we at least drive by U-C-L-Ayyy?" Jenny clutched my wife's headrest.

"Honey," Suzy said, "This is a piece of American history in the making. Maybe you can't appreciate this right now, but this is a once-in-a-lifetime experience. And one day, you'll tell your grandchildren all about it."

I flipped on the radio and tuned in to an oldies station playing that familiar trumpet intro to Johnny Cash's *Ring of Fire.*

"Love is a burning thing," I dropped my chin and sang along with The Man in Black: *"And it makes, a fiery ring."*

"When are we going to eat-" Billy asked.

"Later!" I snapped—damn kid made me miss a line. *"I fell into a ring of fire.* Dum-dum-dum *I fell into a burnin' ring of fire. I went down, down, down, and the flames rose higher."*

"Can't we stop at Denny's?"

"Later! *-And it burns, burns, burns..."*

I didn't see the traffic slowing down and I slammed on the brakes.

"And it burns, burns, burns..."

"I think there's an accident," Suzy said.

"Shhhhitttt," I hissed, looking at my watch. 7 AM. I wanted to get there at eight to avoid the crowd, but I knew we'd never make it by then. We crept up to a cop waving traffic along. An upside-down red Chevette leaned up against the divider. It's top was caved in.

"The ring of fire? The ring of FIRE."

"Oooh, look, New Jersey!" Jenny cried in glee over the trumpets. She had hoped to see a license plate from every state while we were on vacation.

I slowed up as we passed to get in on my fair share of rubbernecking. An EMS worker sat on the divider, smoking a cigarette while two others loaded a covered body into the back of an ambulance. A second body lay under a white sheet on the side of the road.

"Oh my Lord," Suzy gasped.

"Whoa!" Billy crawled over Jenny and pawed the window.

"Sit down!" I blindly reached around and yanked Billy by the neck across the back seat. "Don't look! DO NOT LOOK!"

"But we haven't seen a license plate from New Jersey, yet," Jenny protested. In the rearview mirror, I could see her scratching off Jersey on her list.

An hour later, the Chevy chugged up Sunset Boulevard. We passed a drugstore and I asked Suzy if we had enough film.

"I bought two fresh rolls."

"Two rolls? I guess that should do it."

"I've got the disposable camera for a backup," she said.

"There it is!" I pointed out the green overhead sign. I flipped on my left turn blinker, but the entire street was blocked with a section of highway divider bearing an orange and black ROAD CLOSED sign.

"Shhhhittt!" I pounded the wheel. "I should've known the street'd be blocked off."

"Let me look at the street map," Suzy said.

"I don't need a map. I'll find it." We wound through the back streets for an hour, drawing dirty stares from the well-heeled residents as I slowed at corners to eye the street signs.

"Are we almost there yet?" Jenny moaned.

"I'm starving!" Billy whined.

"Shut up!" I rounded another corner and spotted a crowd of people. The street was lined with cars and Jenny began madly crossing middle American states off her list.

"We've seen every State except Delaware and Hawaii!"

"Big wup," Billy said.

"We're here!" Suzy announced.

"Can I stay in the car?" Billy droned.

I turned and gave Billy the poker-face I reserved for special moments to let him know that if he made one more sound, I'd snap his neck.

It was just like on TV. The property was lined with a green plastic barrier. And it looked as though an entire trailer park had unloaded on the lawn, standing on both sides of the barrier, snapping pictures.

It took a few minutes to get over the awe of actually being there. Finally I grabbed the camera and turned to Billy. "Take this sandwich knife and stand in front of the spot and make like you're killing your sister," I instructed him.

"But Dad, there's people there."

"Alright!" I called out to the heavy-set pre-teens standing near the spot. "You kids wanna let somebody else have a chance?"

They moped away. Billy's face was beet red.

"You got the knife?"

"Yehhhhssss," he shrugged and Jenny followed him over to the spot. She faced him and exposed her neck and he held the knife over her like in a horror movie.

"Smile, goddamnit!"

They showed their teeth and I snapped seven pictures.

"Alright Jenny! You lie down on your stomach and Billy you stand over her with a foot on her back and grab the back of her hair."

"But *Da*ddy! I'll get all *dirty*!"

"Don't worry, honey!" Suzy piped in. "I've got an extra set of whites for you. Just do as your Father says."

"Be gentle with her, Billy."

She grudgingly dropped to the prone position. Then Billy placed a worn Nike on the small of her back and grabbed her blond ponytail.

"Ouch!"

"Sorry," Billy said.

"Okay, good Billy! Hold the knife right in front of her throat!"

"Like this?" He held it an inch beneath her left ear.

"Perfect! Okay! Smile! No, not you, Billy, just Jenny!"

Billy grunted and I snapped to the end of the roll. Some other tourists even began snapping pictures of the two of them. I changed rolls and dashed over to Billy and gave him the camera. "Okay! Get one of me with your Mother!"

"Oh, no, Robert!"

"Come on, honey! Where's your spunk?"

"Yeah," Jenny chimed in. "Where's your spunk, Mom?"

"Ohhh, all right." Suzy sighed.

I snatched the knife from Billy and helped Suzy lie face-down in front of the spot. I grabbed a fistful of her blond hair and she lifted her head and managed a smile as I put a foot on her back and held the knife in front of her throat.

"You got it, Billy?"

"I think so!"

"Take two more!"

"Got it!"

"Alright! Let's take one of you and your Mother!"

"Oh, Robert!"

"Hang on!"

Billy took my place straddling his Mother's hips and he grabbed her hair and grunted holding the knife in front of her throat.

"Good one, Billy!" I snapped two pictures. "Now take one of me with Jenny!"

"Daddy!"

"Get back on the ground!"

I got on top of Jenny and grabbed her hair, trying not to hurt her. "How's that, Honey?"

hurt her. "How's that, Honey?"

"Just hurry up and finish!" she cried.

Billy snapped a picture and one of the tourists called out in a southern accent, "Hey how 'bout givin sum-body else a chance?"

"Get two more, Billy!"

"Got em!"

"Good!" I helped Jenny up and brushed her off and kissed her forehead. "That wasn't so bad, now, was it Honey?"

"I guess not," she said.

A bunched up line of tourists had formed, ready to take our place. One man had extracted a Rambo knife from a hip sheath. Jesus, what a bunch of copycats. A man wearing a cowboy hat stepped up, but another man with skin burnt the same shade as his Budweiser tanktop pushed his corpulent wife face-down in front of the spot, before the cowboy hat could set up shop. The woman's cottage cheese thighs flopped against the pavement, bearing a road map of varicose veins traveling up into the legs of her cutoff Wrangler shorts. She groaned and rolled over and blood spilled from her left knee right in the same spot where so much blood had been hosed down to the gutter. Her husband crouched down next to her to survey the damage.

"Hoooweee, we got blood!"

"Get that pig outta there!" the cowboy hat called. "I was first!"

"What'd you call mah wife?" the Bud tanktop stepped up to the cowboy hat. The cowboy hat's hands twitched. He didn't say anything. A loose circle of children nervously ringed the two men.

"You call mah wife a *pig*?" The Bud tanktop's burnt face grew redder.

"I was first!" The cowboy hat repeated in a shaky voice.

The Bud tanktop landed a meaty fist with a thud squarely

and he spun 270 degrees before his knees buckled and he crashed to the ground. Two children shrieked with high-pitched terror while five or six others looked on wide-eyed. The Bud tanktop went down for the cowboy hat and three men tried to stop him, which started a new fight between the Bud tanktop and one of the peacemakers and then *that* fight segued into a third scuffle when someone tried to break it up. Another tourist rushed his wife before the spot and snapped a few pictures and then someone pushed him out of the way and that started another brawl. Some other tourists jockeyed for a photo op in front of the spot while others took pictures and videos of the various scuffles amid the wailing screaming children. I whisked my family away just as two blue-light specials, sirens blaring, pulled up to the curb.

"GET IN THE GODDAMNED CAR!" I screamed.

They hustled inside and I pulled away, stopping after a block to examine the action in the rearview.

"Oooh look! Delaware!" Jenny cooed.

"They're making everybody leave!" Billy said.

"The only one I haven't seen is Hawaii!"

"Yeah like you're gonna see a license plate from Haw*aïi*," Billy said.

"We saw one from Alaska."

"You can *drive* to Alaska, stupid."

"Don't call your sister stupid," I said, feeling a little high, wondering if the scuffle would make the news. I'll bet they'll even say how it started, I thought. They won't believe it back at the office.

I pulled around the corner and a white Mercedes with one-way windows pulled up. A flat hand beckoned me to stop. Shit! I sat up and cleared my throat as I rolled down the window. "Can I help you, sir?"

"Excuse me," a tan skinned man beckoned. "I'm looking for the house where-"

for the house where-"

"Right back there," I laughed, jerking my thumb over my left shoulder, as I exhaled.

"Thanks," the man smiled and hit his power window.

"HAWAII!" Jenny screamed! "They're from Hawaii!"

"No *way*!" Billy spun around to check out the plate.

"Well, how 'bout that?" I said.

"But-" Billy protested.

"You-can-drive-to-Alaska, stupid." Jenny mimicked Billy.

"But Dad," Billy said, "why would anyone ever ship a car from *Hawaii*?"

"If you've got the cash..." I said.

"But that must cost thousands of dollars!"

"Honey," Suzy turned to him. "People with lots of money can do all sorts of things."

Pat Boone's rendition of *Aint That a Shame* came over the radio. I hadn't heard his version in years and I cranked up the volume and hit the pedal to the beat as we wound through the lush streets. As a kid, I always preferred Pat's cover to Fats Domino's original. It was much more upbeat. "*Oh well, Good-bye. Although, I'll cryyyyy. Aint that a shame...*" I crooned along with Pat, examining my cowlicks in the rearview, "*You're the one to blame...*"

"Honey! Look out!" Suzy grabbed my arm. I was veering towards a tree. "Sorry!" I said, patting down the crown of my head. "Alright!" I reached behind me and ruffled Billy's hair. "Let's go to Denny's!" I stepped on the pedal and the Chevy cruised down Sunset.

When I Grow Up to be a Man

The fans spun at high power as the parishioners unstuck their shirts and blouses from their chests, fanning themselves with missalettes through the dead part of the mass. Sitting there, flanked by my parents on either side—the same arrangement devised years ago to prevent rambunctious brothers from laughing and fighting—I felt like a seventeen-year-old weighing down a pony. In the heat, I tried to remind myself that I had a B.S., despite having moved back in with my parents to weather a fruitless job search.

Heads teetered forward and snapped back, eyes popping open and I remembered how I used to go to church with my mother on Saturday nights—another preventive measure designed to keep no more than two children from wreaking havoc in the same mass—and I'd lie down on the pew and conk out, sleeping through the miracle of transubstantiation week after week.

Father Bob rambled on and I swallowed a yawn, noticing Victor in the front row, extending his pinkie, index finger and thumb in the Elvis trident towards the altar. Victor was retarded. He and his elderly parents were a front row fixture at Our Lady by the Sea for as long as I could remember. He was a bear of a man—about six-four, 260. Grey streaks ran through his greased D.A., but he belted out the hymns in the clear tenor of a choir boy. Mass for Victor was like a sporting event. He crooned out the responses, sweating and shifting from foot to foot, while giving the thumbs up to the priest. I remembered an uncomfortable moment years ago, when on the way out of church, he tried to high-five the visiting bishop. Like everyone else, I just tried not to look at him. But I always wondered—sometimes uncomfortably—if he was actually perceiving God while the rest of us practiced geriatric aerobics.

Father Bob's chin fell into his chest and he stuck out his arms and dryly proclaimed,"Lord, hear our prayer."

I grew light-headed in the heat and a distant tinny guitar twanged in my ear, sending an electric surge coursing down my spine. I couldn't sit still and suddenly felt as though I might scream. And I don't exactly remember climbing out of the pew, but suddenly I was standing in front of the altar, arms outstretched Broadway-style, as I belted out the opening line of the Beach Boys' *Fun, Fun, Fun.*

"WELL, SHE'S GOT HER DADDY'S CAR AND SHE'S CRUISIN' TO THE HAMBURGER *STAND* NOW!"

I duck-walked a line in front of the altar, my head spinning as though I teetered on the edge of a cliff. My eyes coasted over the parishioners, glued to the pew, as though they were dining at McDonalds and I whipped out an AK-47. And in the cozy crescent arrangement of pews in Our Lady by the Sea, there wasn't a bad seat in the house.

"SEEMS SHE FORGOT ALL ABOUT THE LIBRARY LIKE SHE TOLD HER OLD *MAN* NOWWWWW!"

The base line pumped in my ears and they sat transfixed by my performance in a way the most eloquent priest could only dream of. Church-going Catholics will attend more than three thousand masses over the course of their lives, all of them lumped together in a collective mush of dutiful boredom. But this was one mass they would never forget.

"SHE'S GOT THE RADIO BLASTIN' AND SHE'S CRUISIN' JUST AS FAST AS SHE *CAN* NOW!"

Victor stared at me with a glint in his eye and began stomping his feet in time.

"AND WE'LL HAVE FUN, FUN, FUN, TIL HER DADDY TAKES HER T-BIRD AWAYYYYYYYYYYY!"

The parishioners were statues.

"AH-WHOOOOOOOO! AH-WHOOOOO-HOOOOO-HOO-HOO-HOOOOOOOO! FUN! FUN! TIL HER DADDY TAKES HER T-BIRD A-WHOOOOOOOO...."

I would have treated them to a second verse, but the guitar faded in my ear and the rush coursing through my head slowed to a sugary stop. My voice broke, but I continued to hear the words until I realized that Victor had taken over the rest of the chorus, right on key and clear as a bell. It was as though we had eluded the collective zap from some giant PAUSE button. But then his mother cracked him on the shoulder and he stopped singing. My head dropped and my hands felt funny at my sides. I looked up at the stone faces, unable to move until a man rose from the pew. Pink and blue veins coursed through his forehead down to his bulbous purple-pocked nose. A pot belly slumped over the belt of his golf slacks, straining as he extended his arm, pointing his finger at me like a gun.

"WHAT IN THE HELL DO YOU THINK YOU'RE *DOING*?!"

His wife bit her lip and locked her head forward while his son and daughter looked up wide-eyed at the quivering lip of their father.

"Robert, please," his wife said, placing her palms on his shirt.

"I'm sorry, Suzy," he said, smoothing down his greased cowlicks before turning back towards me. "BUT I WOULD LIKE TO KNOW JUST WHAT IN THE HELL THIS YOUNG MAN THINKS HE'S *DOING?!*"

I glanced over at my own father, studying me with a look of stoic hurt, while my mother's eyes sagged with nervous concern. Then my gaze shifted to Victor. He gave me a thumbs up and a wink, and a chill raced through me as though a dozen bees just lit off my forehead. I swallowed hard and walked out of the church with the swift gait of a speckled hit-man pacing out of a barber shop. I didn't stop moving until I reached the water.

The falling crests rolled in silver and blue and my stomach knotted as I stared down at the spent waves crumbling at my feet and sliding back. I felt bad for ruining the mass. But I kept wondering if I was the only person who ever felt a compulsion to scream out in church. Even to shout "Amen!" or "Time-Out!" or anything to spice up the unfeeling monotony of the whole affair. At least I gave them something new to talk about over breakfast, I thought, breathing in the salty air and feeling the sun wash over my face. I bent over and picked up a heart-sized stone, weighing it in my hand. It was heavy. I shut my eyes and spun 360 degrees, hucking it as hard as I could. It tumbled in the air like a badly thrown football, failing to traverse half as many waves as I imagined. My feet began to sink in the sand and I felt the rumble in my gut and turned to go back to the church parking lot, still feeling a pang of guilt for my parents, who were forced to endure the outbreaks of their pariah son.

I found the car, but my dad had the keys. The air grew fuzzy and I experienced a familiar anxiety: While I was certainly no longer a boy, my lack of independence didn't allow me to feel like a man. I had spent almost a year under the post-graduate man-boy purgatory of my parents' roof, working the $6.55 an hour job I had worked all through college, and I wondered how much longer I had to go.

The organ came to life and I glanced at my watch—the Communion hymn. I recognized the droning intro to *I am the Bread of Life,* the words of which came straight out of the Book of John:

"I am the Bread of Life.
You who come to Me shall not hunger.
And who believes in me shall not thirst.
No one-"

"AH-WHOOOOOOOO! AH-WHOOOOO-HOOOOO-HOO-HOO-HOOOOOOOO-" The church door flew open and Victor strutted out carrying the Beach Boys' chorus in his clear falsetto. "-FUN! FUN! TIL HER DADDY TAKES HER T-BIRD AH-WHOOOOOOOO...."

His mother cracked him again on his massive shoulder.

"*Victor!* Get in the car!"

She disregarded my look of apology as she palmed his head under the roof of the back seat.

"Go with it, dude," he said, extending his thumbs up sign out the window.

"Jesus," I said to myself, folding my arms and leaning against the passengers' side of the car. I gazed up at a white gull sitting atop the crossbar of the steeple until it fell from its perch, gliding out over the crests of the silver waves and disappearing in the pink sky. I glanced back at the church and kicked at the gravel as I waited for Mass to let out.

ORDER FORM

This form can also be downloaded from the Silk City website: www.ziplink.net/~jblesso

To order copies of **OFF TO A BAD START: Chicken Soup for the Sold**, check your local bookstore, or mail this order form with payment to:

Silk City Press
225 Washington St.
Suite 1
Hoboken, NJ 07030

Please enclose $12.95 plus $3 postage and handling for one copy. Add $1 per additional copy. The following discount applies to multiple orders.

# of copies	percent discounted	total (incl. P&H + disc.)	add sales tax (NJ res. only)
1	—	**$15.95**	.78
2	20%	**$24.72**	1.25
3	20%	**$36.08**	1.87
4	30%	**$42.26**	2.18
5	40%	**$45.85**	2.33
50+	50%	*	

***For bulk orders, or for information on author visit or interview, call or fax Silk City Press at (201) 798-7312**

Send me ______ copies of *OFF TO A BAD START: Chicken Soup for the Sold.* Enclosed is a check or money order for ______. *NJ residents please add 6% sales tax.*

Name: ____________________________________

Address: ____________________________________

City, State, Zip: ____________________________________

Tel: ____________________________________

E-mail: ____________________________________

ORDER FORM

This form can also be downloaded from the Silk City website: www.ziplink.net/~jblesso

To order copies of **OFF TO A BAD START: Chicken Soup for the Sold**, check your local bookstore, or mail this order form with payment to:

Silk City Press
225 Washington St.
Suite 1
Hoboken, NJ 07030

Please enclose $12.95 plus $3 postage and handling for one copy. Add $1 per additional copy. The following discount applies to multiple orders.

# of copies	percent discounted	total (incl. P&H + disc.)	add sales tax (NJ res. only)
1	—	**$15.95**	.78
2	20%	**$24.72**	1.25
3	20%	**$36.08**	1.87
4	30%	**$42.26**	2.18
5	40%	**$45.85**	2.33
50+	50%	*	

***For bulk orders, or for information on author visit or interview, call or fax Silk City Press at (201) 798-7312**

Send me ______ copies of *OFF TO A BAD START: Chicken Soup for the Sold.* Enclosed is a check or money order for ______. *NJ residents please add 6% sales tax.*

Name: ______________________________

Address: ______________________________

City, State, Zip: ______________________________

Tel: ______________________________

E-mail: ______________________________

ORDER FORM

This form can also be downloaded from the Silk City website: www.ziplink.net/~jblesso

To order copies of **OFF TO A BAD START: Chicken Soup for the Sold**, check your local bookstore, or mail this order form with payment to:

Silk City Press
225 Washington St.
Suite 1
Hoboken, NJ 07030

Please enclose $12.95 plus $3 postage and handling for one copy. Add $1 per additional copy. The following discount applies to multiple orders.

# of copies	percent discounted	total (incl. P&H + disc.)	add sales tax (NJ res. only)
1	—	**$15.95**	.78
2	20%	**$24.72**	1.25
3	20%	**$36.08**	1.87
4	30%	**$42.26**	2.18
5	40%	**$45.85**	2.33
50+	50%	*	

***For bulk orders, or for information on author visit or interview, call or fax Silk City Press at (201) 798-7312**

Send me ______ copies of *OFF TO A BAD START: Chicken Soup for the Sold.* Enclosed is a check or money order for ______. *NJ residents please add 6% sales tax.*

Name: ________________________________

Address: ________________________________

City, State, Zip: ________________________________

Tel: ________________________________

E-mail: ________________________________